DE GAULLE

DE GAULLE

François Mauriac

Translated from
the French by
RICHARD HOWARD

1966

DOUBLEDAY & COMPANY, INC.

GARDEN CITY, NEW YORK

DE GAULLE

I

THE HISTORY of a man is the history of an age. "Thirty years in the life of the world"—*there* is the subtitle for a biography of Charles de Gaulle, and I do not contemplate it without apprehension. Like bogus novels, amateur histories fill the bookshops, and I shall not try to deceive my readers or pretend to be equipped for such an undertaking.

The fact remains that for these thirty years I have thought of General de Gaulle in a certain way. This way is the whole subject of my book. I repeat this in order to reassure myself —as if my view of De Gaulle could be separated from what he has done! Hence I shall constantly be measuring myself against the very history I shall not write.

Then what shall I do? Nothing but consider my model, continue to devour him with my eyes, as I have done since 1944, and dream of him aloud, as I did during the Occupation—for a share of dreams subsists in all our relations with him. The myth De Gaulle constituted for us during the four years of the Resistance has never entirely vanished.

This is not to say that he obsesses us, or that I am incapable of a disinterested judgment about him, as some accuse me of being. I have continually criticized him since 1940— and sometimes altered some of my criticisms. For example, in the case of the Rassemblement du Peuple Français to which I was opposed, I shall show, in the proper place, how I appeared to be in the right—and yet, on an essential point,

I was blind. I have never stopped observing De Gaulle with a curiosity, an interest that is the very opposite of the trance I am said to fall into whenever he is mentioned. It is, to be sure, an interest steeped in anxiety because the history is not completed, because I do not know the final chapter, and because Brutus and Cassius crouch in the shadows of this great destiny.

I am not writing a history but first of all attempting to draw a portrait with lines, shading, retouches, second thoughts—nothing like a logical and reasoned plan. And when the countenance appears as I conceive it, I shall turn, in Part II, to De Gaulle himself and investigate his own texts (including some of the least known) until I have found a confirmation by De Gaulle himself of the way in which I have thought of him since the first day we lunched together, September 1, 1944, in the rue Saint-Dominique.

The mist that concealed him in the days when he was no more than a voice jammed by the enemy's parasites has never entirely cleared: "London here! General de Gaulle speaking . . ." That was at Malagar, in the dead of the blackest winter of all our lives. In our cellar, we listened to the boots of the German officer pounding overhead.

The last image of the mythical De Gaulle appears in a page I wrote in Vémars, Seine-et-Oise, on August 19, 1944. It was published in *Figaro* on August 24, in one of the first issues after the Liberation, under the heading "Le premier des nôtres." A tearful voice read this page over the radio to the sound of the bells of Paris, and while I listened, while I listened to my own words, German soldiers retreating from Le Bourget filled the garden, entered the house. If I pause over this anecdote, it is to suggest that the vision of the mythical De Gaulle was yielding to another which still endures.

On August 30, Vémars was liberated. The last night I had sought refuge in the house of my neighbor Émile

Roche, who had taken me in and given me his own room. On August 31, my two sons, sent by General de Gaulle, called for me in the presidential car. Soldiers were still removing mines from the Le Bourget road. As I remember it, we were going directly from Vémars to the rue Saint-Dominique, where I was to dine with the general. But Claude Mauriac's diary is categorical: it was on September 1, 1944, that this luncheon took place and I first saw the hero no longer merely in my imagination but face to face.

I insert here a few lines from "Le premier des nôtres," as a portrait from memory of the mythical De Gaulle who was to be replaced by the man I waited for, heart pounding, that morning of September 1, my eyes fixed on the door he would push open. Here is the beginning of the page that created quite a stir at the time:

At the saddest hour of our destiny, the hope of France was embodied in one man; it was expressed by the voice of that man —and of that man alone. How many Frenchmen, in those days, came to share his solitude, having understood what it means *to give oneself to France?* Dead or alive, the obscure workers of those first hours will always be embodied for us by the leader who had summoned them, and whom they gave up everything to follow, while so many others waited to see which way the wind would blow, pursued their own interests, and turned traitor. It is to him, to them, that France, ungagged, offers her first cry; released from the stake, it is to him, to them, that she holds out her poor hands. She remembers: Vichy had condemned this man to death *in absentia*. The young French leader who had been the first in Europe to define the conditions of modern warfare was condemned by an old marshal who had been blind for twenty years. The lackeys of the French press, in the executioner's service, covered him with insults and mockery. But we, during those bitter winter nights, kept our ears glued to the radio, while the steps of the German officer shook the ceiling overhead. We listened, fists clenched, and did not restrain our tears. We ran to tell the other members of the family: "General de Gaulle is going to speak, he's speaking now!" At the peak of the Nazi triumph, everything that we see coming true today was announced by that prophetic voice . . .

"The general will come . . ." Can anyone who has not lived, suffered, and, if not fought, at least resisted in some obscure fashion in occupied France, without once crossing the demarcation line, as in my case—can such a person understand that I had to lean against the wall to keep from faltering? But that was my last "trance." A few moments later, sitting opposite General de Gaulle at his own table, I looked at him, I observed him as I was henceforth to continue to do, abashed and yet fascinated, no longer "under the spell"—on the contrary, freed from the spell expressed in "Le premier des nôtres"—but caught up in the project of a mastermind. Even so the project was not formally or even seriously discussed with me that morning in a Paris barely liberated. If only I had written down what was said during that first luncheon! If my son Claude had been present, I would now be able to recapture all of it. What disconcerted me was that the drama then taking place was scarcely touched on. Who would have believed it? De Gaulle questioned me about André Gide! He was concerned about the Académie française, about the empty seats to be filled. I realized that for this man the liberation of Paris must, of course, have been an essential moment but one that he did not consider apart from the period we had lived through since June 1940, or the period still to be lived through until the nation was re-established in its power and its glory.

I should have liked to know, that morning, what the general thought the chances were of amalgamating the French Forces of the Interior, the Francs-Tireurs Partisans, with the Regular Army; of controlling the country when all his forces were fighting at the side of the Allies; of France being present on the day of reckoning.

I myself belonged at the time to the Front national; inevitably I had found myself entangled in that Communist-controlled organization. I would have had something to say about its tactics . . . but no: De Gaulle wanted to talk about André Gide and the Académie française! I was a writer and that, of course, mattered to him. If De Gaulle prides himself on anything in this world, it is on being, himself, a French writer. No doubt he would be quite capable of voicing Louis XVIII's phrase about Chateaubriand: "One must take care to entrust nothing to such men, they would ruin everything . . ." But he would not utter it in the same scornful tone, or even with a hint of disdain, for no element of the glory of France counts more with him than her writers. But they are not usable, as a financier or a jurist is usable. I don't know whether André Malraux has ever dared tell the general that it would have suited him, André Malraux, best, not to clean up the monuments of Paris or to inaugurate museums, but to be Minister of the Interior.

What I found, in that first meeting with General de Gaulle, was not the disdain of all other men that his enemies attribute to him, but the narrow, unbridgeable gulf between them and himself, created not by the pride of self-conscious greatness, but by the calm certainty that he is the State and, it is not too much to say, France herself.

Louis XIV may never have said, "L'État, c'est moi." And if Mme du Barry was in the habit of calling Louis XV, "La France," that was the people's expression for the king. As for myself, a professional "observer of the human heart," I was sitting opposite someone who did not distinguish himself from France, who said, openly, "I am France," without anyone in the world saying he was mad. I was not sorry, that day, to feel somewhat remote from this strange figure, to have nothing to do but keep my eyes and ears open. I had invented many characters, but, believe me, I had never seen one, really seen one with my own eyes, as they say. And this one was sitting here before me at last, both myth and flesh, Shakespearean and contemporary, simultaneously alive, historical, and legendary. I would be quite comfortable, in the best seats in the house, to follow him closely through the whole last act of the play whose first scenes had reached me only as distorted echoes.

For the same reasons, during the first days after our luncheon, I saw the birth of the misunderstanding that still persists between General de Gaulle and Resistance fighters of various political allegiances. The slight distance between him and ourselves to which I, not belonging to any particular parliamentary fauna, accommodated myself quite easily, the gulf that cannot be bridged by familiarities or thumps on the back, that gulf already stretched between De Gaulle and the political parties, as it stretches today.

In the Front national, to which I belonged willy-nilly because my particular Resistance network had been pledged to it, there were scandalized comments on the general's rejection of a young syndicalist Resistance fighter, Louis Saillant, who had hoped to receive certain favors. The flat statement that unions were not to meddle in affairs of State, not even to ask questions was all the Resistance fighter for all his influence in syndicalist circles got from De Gaulle; and it was enough to stupefy and outrage the little world that was the swarming residue of the still tenacious Third Republic.

What these politicians and militants did not understand was that De Gaulle kept the same distance between himself and Churchill, between himself and Roosevelt. He had no sense of social or even personal superiority over them; he was asserting a sovereign authority, an essential autonomy—not that of a man, but that of the State, and more than of the State, of the nation.

This gap, which he maintained between himself and any individuals, any groups that were not "the people" (the people in the village squares and on the roads of France), was made quite clear to me on September 12, 1944, at the Palais de Chaillot, during the meeting organized by the Comité national de la Résistance, now for the first time officially convened around General de Gaulle, in a smoking Paris where the barricades still stood. We were prepared to weep! De Gaulle would, of course, evoke those who had been tortured and shot. What a cry for vengeance would go up! Nothing of the kind: the general quickly passed over the entire emotional side of the situation. He loathes sentimentality, this Frenchman from Lille. And we, the soft-hearted, we felt a chill, and none of us knew what to do with his handkerchief. Any man but De Gaulle would have transformed this encounter of the first Resistance fighter in France with the Resistance into an occasion for self-congratulation, for general conciliation. But De Gaulle proceeded straight to the most burning questions, those that most divided the French Left: the militias, the French Forces of the Interior and the Francs-Tireurs Partisans, must be incorporated by force into the Regular Army; our allies must be convinced that they were wrong to treat France with the disdain that Yalta would manifest to the world.

We had supposed that De Gaulle would address us as survivors of the battle in the shadows that had lasted four years, but he could not have been less concerned. What obsessed him that day, what alone counted, was what still obsesses him today, after twenty years: to convince our allies of what is always due to the France that is eternal. In 1964, as I write this, De Gaulle is still proving to Roosevelt's ghost that there is nothing to be gained by seeking to bypass France, and that Yalta would cost him dear.

What the men of the Resistance gathered at Chaillot had suffered seemed to interest De Gaulle no more than what he himself had suffered and was still to suffer. Nothing mattered less to him than gushing over the past. To give one's life for France—that was the least one could do, and what was the good of discussing it? To remake the State; to remake the Army, to make war, to force the Allies' hand so that France might stand beside them in occupied Germany and at her capitulation—that alone mattered. For the rest, let the dead bury the dead!

An icy wind blew over our hearts. Our disappointment was made up of all the tears we had not shed. As for those whose profession was politics, who constituted the fauna of committees and congresses, they discovered what was to be their tragedy. This meteoric general, the product of Saint-Cyr and the École de Guerre, seemed to them the incarnation of all that was most hateful: the absolute preponderance of the State, the cult of the nation, the indifference to ideologies, the mistrust of political parties, plus an antagonism to them personally and a determination to dominate, to defy, and, if possible, to destroy them. The professional politicians understood on that day that this man would be their tragedy. This staff of iron would not bend. They would have to take him or leave him, as we say, but the history that began that day, and that is still being made, would come down to this: each time they rejected him, they would be obliged to take him back, on pain of death. This insupportable man was an inevitable man.

This contradiction was woven, that day, into the history of De Gaulle, and he himself was aware of it. In his *War Memoirs,* he notes that he left the Palais de Chaillot with a heart full of doubts:

It is true that as I entered the hall, took my place, and made my speech after Georges Bidault's eloquent introduction, I received ringing ovations. Listening only to the cheers, I might have imagined I was back in the unanimous assemblies of Albert Hall and Brazzaville or among the sympathetic audiences of Algiers, Tunis, and Ajaccio. Yet some varying tonality in the enthusiasm, a kind of self-consciousness in the applause, the signals and significant glances exchanged by the participants, the calculated and composed faces that acknowledged my remarks, reminded me that "politicians," old or new, had many nuances in their approbation. It was apparent that their dealings would be complicated, as they proceeded, by an ever greater number of reservations and conditions.

More than ever, then, I had to seek support from the French people rather than from the "elite" groups which tended to come between us. My popularity was a kind of capital with which I could pay off the disappointments that were inevitable among the ruins (III, p. 9).

"More than ever, then, I had to seek support from the French people rather than from the 'elite' groups which tended to come between us." That is the key sentence of this destiny. There is no other debate between De Gaulle and politicians of all parties: he suppresses them by his mere presence. He has no need of them. They turn into old streetcars, no longer good for anything but the scrap heap, into the flea market, instead of the Matignon or the Ministry of the Interior! What a difference in perspective! For them, the whole problem is to know whether this is a temporary annihilation, linked to De Gaulle's presence, which would mean their return to the fray once he is gone; or whether De Gaulle has definitely scrapped the system that nearly killed France but that, politically, was their life.

De Gaulle did not need the meeting at the Palais de Chaillot to discover their unshakable opposition. Already— in Algiers, in 1943—he had seen the situation for what it was: "Probing their souls," he writes in his *War Memoirs*, apropos of the Consultative Assembly, "I reached a point where I asked myself if among all those who spoke of revolution I was not, in truth, the only revolutionary" (II, p. 172).

He is the only revolutionary; and the revolution he demands proceeds from no ideology. Hence it antagonizes all the ideologists of the Left, and all the ideologists of the

Right. The revolution he demands and will conduct against wind and tide (and what winds, what tides!) is linked to the conditions of France's survival—conditions inimical to a political generation trained by the Third Republic and directed by the traditional parties.

This is the moment to ask the question: "Who is this man who is stronger than all those allied against him?" A prophet who imagines himself entrusted with a mission from on high? No; this Christian has not heard voices. He has believed before the event—and he has verified his belief when the event took place—that the character of the man he was would dominate the event, whatever it might be. He has known that his character would be his fate.

I turn back to *The Edge of the Sword*, first published in 1932, though most of its pages consist of three lectures given at the École supérieure de la Guerre in 1927 by Captain de Gaulle: "The Conduct of War and the Leader," "Of Character," "Of Prestige." Thirteen years before the catastrophe that was unforeseeable and indeed unimaginable at the time, this young leader of thirty-seven knew in advance what he would do and what he would be.

Throughout his public life, he will take into account only what exists; the analysis of reality, unvitiated by prejudice, constitutes his strength. But reality is also his own nature, the character of Charles de Gaulle, whose possibilities escape him no more than the rest: the character that will necessitate his fate.

I ponder over this young leader who, in 1927, was as much a writer as I myself; who had been a child, an adolescent, who must have suffered, who must have loved and been loved, who prayed, who had an idea of God and of man's relations with God: not a line of what he has written, to my knowledge, concerns this unknown man. Perhaps he revealed something of himself in the letter to his friend Louis Nachin, written when he left the command of the 19th

Rifle Battalion at Trèves in 1929: "Ah, the bitterness one feels these days about wearing a uniform in peacetime! Yet it must be done. In a few years, people will be clinging to my coattails to save the country . . ." This exclamation of prophetic pride concerns the country, not his destiny as an individual. As early as 1927, it is as if he no longer has a private history (though of course he did have one).

If since the Romantic period, a man of letters has been first of all a man who reveals himself, Charles de Gaulle is certainly not a man of letters. Either he has never been tempted, as the rest of us have since Montaigne, to make himself the subject of his works, or his concept of himself as an historical figure has absorbed the private man, so that very early in life he could no longer dissociate himself from France and eventually could no longer regard himself separately.

Certainly this is not surprising, or at least it can be understood, if we start from June 18, 1940. Taking refuge abroad, a madman imagined he was France, and the world believed him because it was true, because his assertion, which appeared to be that of a madman, actually proceeded from an analysis of reality. But thirteen years earlier, when this captain had no prospect but that of a normal military career, there is no doubt—and this is the strange thing—that he had a presentiment, that he was conscious of his destiny.

If he did not then yield to an inclination to confide, to reveal himself, it is because at that very moment a single passion dominated all the others he had ever had, if indeed he had ever had any. That passion was France—not France as she was loved by a follower of Maurras or by a man of the Left, as the incarnation of certain ideas; not the France of the Revolution, nor the France of the monarchy—but France as she has been created by a thousand years of history, France as she is, so precious and so imperiled, who has been given no promise of eternity, whom geography has made an easy prey to the lusts of the German invader,

and whom the bad political customs of her people have
condemned to party division and mortal instability of government. As early as *The Edge of the Sword*, there was no
longer any history for this captain to write except the history of this one love.

There was a time—and that time lasted almost all my life
—when the prestige of a writer seemed to me greater than
any other, not only the prestige of the creator of a world,
like Balzac or Proust, but even of an author of confessions,
like André Gide and most others of my profession. But I
discover, as I reach the end of my life, and as I observe De
Gaulle, that I see everything from another perspective. No
sooner had Gide, whom I so greatly admired, gone to his
rest than his *oeuvre* crumbled before my eyes and I sought
vainly in it for what had seduced me for so many years; all
that remained was his obsession with an abnormality glori-
fied and sublimated, the preponderance of the sexual.

As I left the luncheon on September 1, 1944, where De
Gaulle, whom I was seeing for the first time, so surprised
me by mentioning Gide, in that still-smoldering Paris, I experienced a reversal of my values; I now saw true greatness (sanctity aside) in the glory of a man who identified
himself with his people, and not in the fame of a man who
identified himself with his abnormality. In the course of my
long life, no public man before De Gaulle, seen from a distance or at close range, had provoked this reversal in me.
It is true that I knew Marshal Lyautey, for instance, only at
the very end of his life, when he was no longer anything
more than an old lion whose roars were ridiculous. I never
met Clemenceau. Yet in the light of De Gaulle's example—
a De Gaulle without soldiers, without popular mandate,
obscure and unknown, in a sense a man born of a shameful
disaster, flung upon the shores of England by a horrible tide,
who nonetheless held his own against two illustrious con-
querors, Winston Churchill and Franklin Roosevelt—in the

light of this example I understood why I had been disappointed at Versailles in 1919 by Clemenceau, leader of a victorious France and the world's most powerful army, who still had not been able to stand up to Woodrow Wilson and to Lloyd George, two very small men compared to Churchill and to Roosevelt.

I do not fall into a trance before De Gaulle, but it is true that ever since that first luncheon I have had a new sense of what constitutes true greatness and true glory.

What is it? What was so strange, so singular, about this provisionally appointed brigadier general, who turned dissident in 1940 and was to be condemned to death for this crime?

Since the Liberation, whether he has taken the helm or voluntarily abjured it, whether in the rue Saint-Dominique, at Colombey-les-Deux-Églises, at the Matignon, or in the Élysée, his power has remained, the power he possessed in London, in Algiers, the power that was to break the will of the omnipotent Roosevelt. A power based on what? General de Gaulle is not a genius, in the sense in which General Bonaparte was a genius. The term, moreover, seems too vague for a mind that is the opposite of vague. That his character was his fate, he realized clearly from the beginning, and even thirteen years before the beginning. The thirty-seven-year-old captain knew by which characteristics of his nature he was to dominate life.

To an old man like myself, if he looks back over his life, the part played by chance seems very great, whatever the proportion of will and courage! An old man measures what he owes to the circumstances that have influenced his fate and that have decided everything. De Gaulle is the sole example I know of a man who, while he was still young and still obscure, thirteen years before history took him for its own, defined with baffling precision what he must be in order to master events then unforeseeable, whose horror no one could conceive in 1927. For at that time another still-obscure man, Adolf Hitler, had not yet left the wings, or, if he was already crossing the stage, still seemed no more than a supernumerary, perhaps even a comic one.

The chapter in *The Edge of the Sword* entitled "Of Character" is a strange case of prophecy achieved solely by self-scrutiny: by analyzing himself, this French officer simultaneously analyzed the circumstances that, after 1940, would henceforth make him indispensable to his people, as he had predicted to Louis Nachin in 1929.

This was not a matter of mystical inspiration, but of observation: "Such as I am, I cannot fail to be, at a given moment, in the center of the stage." He discerned an inescapable correspondence between the strength he possessed, linked to what he calls "character," and the destiny of a victorious and apparently omnipotent nation, which was, beginning however, to slip from its eminence; and De Gaulle's simplifying mind had already noted and recorded the political reasons for this fatal decline.

No, there was nothing mystical in this soldier, a master of analysis who derived his foresight both from what he observed outside, and what he acknowledged inside, himself: the strength that filled him to overflowing, and the weakness of peoples and their assemblies; the love inside himself, which gave everything to France, and outside, private interests which combine and conflict with one another.

Of course he believed in his star; but he knew his star's reasons. He multiplied "character" tenfold in himself by the study he made of it, by the daily exercise of his gifts:

Was not what Alexander called "his hope," Caesar "his luck," and Napoleon "his star" simply the fact that they knew they had a particular gift of making contact with realities closely enough to dominate them? For those who are greatly gifted this faculty often shines through their personalities. There may be nothing in itself exceptional about what they say or their way of saying it,

but other men in their presence have the impression of a natural
force destined to master events. Flaubert expresses this feeling
when he describes the still adolescent Hannibal as already
clothed "in the undefinable splendor of those who are destined
for great enterprises" (*The Edge of the Sword,* p. 22).

This is not the least striking feature of the young leader
of 1927, who in that year foresaw both that he would dominate others and that he would not be loved by them, or at
least, that if he were loved, he would neither have sought
nor desired it. Indeed the price of his mastery of events,
which we have already mentioned but to which we must
return, is the distance from others, the gap that makes De
Gaulle odious to a certain group born of a century and a
half of parliamentarianism, but not to the French people,
the masses who participate in greatness only through a
great man like this one. As for himself, he needs these
masses, needs the direct contact with them in order to
charge himself, as a battery is charged. The French people
are not humiliated by this man who could do nothing without them, without being in direct contact with them. On
the other hand, the political fauna swarming on the surface
of events will never forgive De Gaulle for the gap, the difference in level, which also implies a change of tone in the
words exchanged.

It is easy to understand why the French President of
1964 sets himself apart in this lofty solitude—for twenty
years he has had to go alone through so many ordeals, over
so many abysses, before crossing the threshold of the Élysée
Palace. But I find it astonishing that the captain of 1927
should have chosen from that moment on not to please but
to withdraw and keep his distance, as if he knew in advance that he had been singled out and designated for his
role:

Furthermore, powerful personalities equipped with the qualities needed in the fighting soldier, and capable of standing up to

the tests of great events, frequently lack that surface charm which wins popularity in ordinary life. Strong characters are, as a rule, rough, disagreeable, and aggressive. The man in the street may, somewhat shyly, admit their superiority and pay them lip service, but they are not often liked and, therefore, seldom favored. . . . The man of character incorporates in his own person the severity inherent in his effort. This is felt by his subordinates, and at times they groan under it. In any event, a leader of this quality is inevitably aloof, for there can be no authority without prestige, and no prestige unless he keeps his distance. Those under his command mutter in whispers about his arrogance and the demands he makes. But once action starts, criticism disappears (*The Edge of the Sword*, pp. 34 and 42).

That the most highly regarded captain of his generation ("He was the best!" Marshal Pétain said, even in Vichy) was already determined *not to please*, to remain alone, not out of misanthropy or because he was so inclined but because domination implies solitude, is astonishing enough— though less so than another idea that he envisaged and pondered from this moment on, that he almost caressed— an idea most likely to shock, to scandalize the circles in which he moved: the idea that a soldier must know how to disobey. Yet that is what Captain de Gaulle thought and that is what he wrote; I suppose that the passage from *The Edge of the Sword* in which he expressed it had already been part of the lecture he gave at the École de Guerre. He published it, in any case, eight years before June 18, 1940. In it he said: "Those who achieve something great must often pass beyond the appearances of a false discipline . . ." He cited the examples of Pélissier at Sevastopol, of Lanrezac after Charleroi, of Lyautey. He recalled the judgment of the First Sea Lord, Admiral Fisher, on Admiral Jellicoe: "He has all Nelson's qualities but one: he doesn't know how to disobey!"

Would he have been surprised, this potential dissident of 1927 and 1932, if by some miracle his imminent destiny had

been revealed to him; if he had found himself transported
to Clermont-Ferrand on Friday, August 2, 1940; if he had
heard Army Corps General Frère, commanding the Twelfth
Region and presiding over the military tribunal (Generals
de la Laurencie and de la Porte Du Theil were among the
judges) condemn ex-General Charles de Gaulle to military
degradation, to the confiscation of his property, and to
death? What would the author of *The Edge of the Sword*
have felt if it had been revealed to him that on December 8,
1940, he would lose his citizenship?

This horrible series of events started on June 22 of that
same year: by ministerial decision, the promotion of Charles
de Gaulle to the rank of brigadier general was canceled.
On June 26, at the instigation of General Weygand, an
order of inquiry against Charles de Gaulle was followed by
a charge of disobedience in the presence of the enemy and
provocation to mutiny. The military tribunal of the Seven-
teenth Region, convening in Toulouse, on that day condemned Charles de Gaulle to four years in prison and a
fine of one hundred francs.

Had the author of *The Edge of the Sword* learned in 1932
of these two judgments without knowing the circumstances that were to provoke them, one might imagine his
deciding: "Thus I gambled, and thus I lost . . ." But that
would not have been his reaction, for despite what is said
about him, no one is less of a gambler than De Gaulle, if a
gambler is a man who trusts entirely to luck. For De Gaulle,
luck lies in the opportunities his own moves present to him.
He is a gambler certainly, if gambling means risking everything; but De Gaulle takes no blind risks, for it is not himself
that is involved: his fortunes are the fortunes of France.

This identification is the share of mysticism and of madness in this singular character, yet here madness joins reality. This gambler cannot lose because the future is invisibly

inscribed in what is happening before his eyes; De Gaulle's
genius lies in his ability to decipher that writing, which is
invisible to other men, and he has almost never made an
error in decoding.

As a matter of fact, De Gaulle has always based his present action on the future events that exist potentially in what
is happening at the time. That is why I can imagine Captain
de Gaulle being quite unmoved by a prophecy that faced
him with a death sentence. I imagine him instead telling
himself: "Nothing can ever cause me to be against France.
I must have escaped my judges, since they condemn me *in
absentia*. It is therefore where I am that France will be."

On November 29, 1940, he was to declare before a London microphone:

Each of us is a man who struggles and who suffers—yes! who
struggles and who suffers—not for himself but for all the others.

De Gaulle did not linger over it, but even so he had
doubtless said more than he intended about his personal
drama. Accused of "treason, endangering state security, and
desertion abroad in wartime," he was condemned *in absentia* on August 2, 1940, to death and to military degradation. On the next day, the general alluded to this in his
broadcast speech:

The enemy is beginning the dismemberment, and completing
the pillage, of the part of French territory he occupies. The old
men saving their skins in Vichy are spending their time and their
passion condemning those guilty of continuing to fight for France.

There was no other trace, at the time, of what De Gaulle
must have been feeling, except perhaps the repetition, four
days later, of the same scornful reference to the "men who
are saving their skins in Vichy", and except these lines:

Duty to France, duty to the Empire, forbid hesitation, false
prudence, cowardly circumspection. In the enormous upheaval,

all that has any meaning or value are men who can think, will, and act according to the terrible rhythm of events. The others will be swept away.

On August 12, he concluded his radio speech:

That is what I have done, that is what I wish to do. Thus I account to the people of France, in whose service I have placed myself once and for all! The enemy and his Vichy accomplices label my conduct and that of the good Frenchmen who have joined me in the battle treason. Nothing encourages us more. For nothing indicates more clearly that our path is the right one.

The end of the next speech, on August 16, shows that he continued to be haunted by the Clermont-Ferrand condemnation:

The way to salvation is victory. Frenchmen look to those who fight to attain it, those whom Marshal Pétain and his followers condemn for treason. Those who fight for victory have a calm spirit and a heart full of hope, for they know that it will soon be clear who has betrayed and who has served France.

He was thinking as much of his comrades as of himself:

October 27, 1940. It is now very clear why and on whose account the men of Vichy pursue, imprison, and condemn to death those who do not resign themselves to infamous servitude.

December 16, 1940. Naturally it is such men whom the Vichy courts pursue with their hatred and their insults. It is such men whom the Vichy courts describe as traitors and condemn to death. It is such men whom the Vichy courts decree to be no longer French!

The De Gaulle of 1927 did not know the outcome of the event whose preambles were then scarcely apparent—but he knew himself. Whatever the event, he would be equal to it. It was the event that was unpredictable, not the character of this man at the height of his powers. That character was a gift of God, and at the same time strengthened day after day by reflection, experience, and the exercise of an inflexible will. He knew then that he was such that, if the event came, he, Charles de Gaulle, would be raised up and carried on the crest of the wave. He noted in 1927 that "Disraeli accustomed himself from adolescence to think as a Prime Minister."

For De Gaulle, even then, infinitely more was involved than occupying first place, and here we come back to his madness—the madness that history was to confirm. I do not claim that in 1927 he already thought: *"Moi, la France!"* But he had identified his individual fate with that of the nation. He would not be great without it, but neither would the nation be great without him. There is no doubt that he classified himself from that moment on among those whom he calls "ambitious for the first rank," whom he tells us "see no other purpose in life than to leave their mark upon events, and who from the shoal where the common days strand them, dream only of the tides of history."

A reader of Chateaubriand, he may have believed he was one of them, but he was slandering himself. He already exceeded them—though he may not have known it—by the loftiness of the love he had vowed not to himself but to France, or to himself, on condition that France and he constitute a single being.

Never, at any moment of his public or private life, has he made use of France. De Gaulle does not identify his own interest with that of the nation with the cunning of an ambitious man, like the two Bonapartes who ruled her. For it was during the nation's deepest misfortune, deepest ruin, deepest shame that his alliance with her was sealed. It is strange to think that it was the instinct to preserve not himself but France that flung him, in June 1940, into an adventure in which, even more than his life, his honor was forfeited. It would have been nothing for this man who had been a soldier in 1914 to risk his life—but to risk his glory in the absolute sense of the word, to risk eternal opprobrium! Yet we have seen the man condemned to death *in absentia* in 1940 face the possibility of the same thing again in Algeria, for after all, the mutinous generals might have triumphed. If De Gaulle had had to submit to the law of a victorious Organization armée secrète his colonels would without doubt have found ammunition against the hated man in the letter that made the Algerian departments part of the French state. Yet the man whom we all saw and heard on the television screen, on a certain evening, denouncing the "two dozen" rebellious generals with calm and complete disdain, made us realize immediately that he himself had no doubt as to the end of the story.

This was indeed the same man who, in June 1940, immediately after his first sentence had been posted in Toulouse, judged and sentenced his judges and sent the men of Vichy to the tribunal before which they appeared in due time, to end as De Gaulle had predicted. This brings us back to the singular quality of De Gaulle as a gambler: he stakes everything on a single card, but never by chance; he always knows both the card and the fact that it is the right one. He takes risks, of course; but no one can calculate probabilities as he can.

As the threat of the disaster grew, he discerned its causes and defined its remedy, but in vain. Between 1934, which saw the publication of the *Army of the Future*, and 1940, it was of no use to De Gaulle to know what had to be done to keep Troy from being destroyed. But once Troy was indeed destroyed, he continued to prophesy over the ruins and described in advance, the invader's ultimate debacle as it did, in fact, occur. The same armored divisions that De Gaulle could not convince the French Army to create destroyed Germany.

Initially, he spoke merely as a soldier determined to set forth accurately the nature of the imminent battle and the conditions of what could have been our victory and was to assure Hitler's. I was wrong to compare De Gaulle to Cassandra. He has never prophesied, never sought the secret of our salvation in a chicken's entrails. No one could be less mystical. What he interprets is always the most intense reality. There is nothing of the seer about him: in 1930 we had the possibility of winning the war. In 1935 there was still time. In 1940 it was too late.

The truth, which his simplifying genius had sifted from the morass of routines—without, alas! convincing the leaders on whom the decision depended—he had first perceived on the terrain itself, the terrain that is the living body of the nation. We must reread the key passage of *The Army of the Future*.

Our decisive battles we wage in clear weather, on a broad plain crossed by roads in good condition. The assailant, having approached under cover of the forests of the Rhineland, the Moselle, and the Ardennes, finding everywhere a terrain permeable to his onslaught, has merely to choose his sites, his moments. The defender, if he remains passive, finds himself surprised, trapped, bypassed, and thus Villeroi collapses at Ramillies, a Bazaine is bottled up in Metz. If, on the contrary, he is mobile, enterprising, like Luxembourg at Fleurus or Napoleon in 1814, he dashes to the necessary points, parries wherever necessary, and seizes the initiative, which is the only fruitful attitude to take towards Germany which, although incomparable in achieving what it has prepared for, loses its means when it is attacked unexpectedly and shows the incapacity to adapt itself to the unforeseen that explains Valmy, Jena, the Marne. Thus it is by maneuvering that France will be protected (pp. 39–40).

The battle that the soldier Charles de Gaulle, the author of *The Army of the Future*, was waging against an immobility symbolized by the Maginot Line—a battle he was to lose—soon obliged him to focus his thoughts on politics, on the political conditions of the disaster he saw taking shape before his eyes, from day to day, almost from hour to hour. What might have been avoided happened for reasons that

De Gaulle alone seemed to discern in France before the cataclysm—a France divided between the Front populaire and the Action française with, in the center, the enormous mass of private interests that are always incapable of reacting to anything that is not immediate. It seems as if, during those years, De Gaulle was the only man in France who did not submit to some ideology, some class or party interest. By refusing to do so he remained as alien to the Right as to the Left.

By the thirties, we can discover the sources of his solitude in a democracy pulverized into parties, the two largest of which, the SFIO (Socialists) and the Communists, promulgated dogmas that forbade all debate but yielded to every electoral and parliamentary opportunism.

Indeed, this professional soldier from a good Catholic family shared with the best men of the Left—the future Resistance fighters—the same Jacobin passion that made France so great between 1792 and 1814. The young leader, said to be a follower of Maurras, excluded no one in past history as he was to exclude no one in the history he came to dominate. Provided France was served, and provided she is served, he asks for no accounting from Frenchmen whatever and however different the banners and standards they serve under may be. His sole mission has always been to *rally* them—he, the most audacious of all, the most revolutionary, the dissident who dared to oppose the legal political power of the country and a glorious marshal of France, the man sentenced to death *in absentia* who, from that day forward, became the judge of his judges, the man beside whom the socialist and communist politicians look like so many circumspect petits bourgeois.

But it is among the Right that De Gaulle has always inspired the most hatred, and with reason. I speak here of a particular Right, for it was, after all, the nationalist and bourgeois masses that supplied a good proportion of the Resistance fighters and furnished the bulk of the RPF troops, and it is these masses that still support De Gaulle on every ballot, despite party slogans. But De Gaulle has been hated from the first by that species of conservative whose political choice is determined by his privileges, who is obsessed by safeguarding those privileges so that he turns communism into a "sacred" beast, to be hunted down whatever the cost; should the Front populaire prevail or threaten to prevail, this kind of conservative welcomes the German occupation and rallies to the Swastika, if that is the only opposition he can find to support.

We now draw a modest veil over things we saw and read in June 1940, over the horrible relief of some, the euphoria that oozed from their writings. I am not identifying such conservatives as these with the honest Rightists who, from Vichy to "Algérie française," offered De Gaulle the "no" of those who see, hear, and understand nothing that is contrary to their bias, and who are often noble beings. The conservative who took a dim and horrible delight in June 1940 belonged to a different breed altogether.

The hatred of communism among those who feared being dispossessed of their property bore no resemblance to De Gaulle's hostility to the Communist Party, whose inexpiable error, as he saw it, was to be dependent on a foreign power and to submit blindly to its directives. There is nothing in common between the visceral hatred of the former and De Gaulle's reasoned hostility—a hostility that is quite capable of abating when the national interest is at stake, and of giving a Thorez a portfolio. This characteristic of De Gaulle's inspires more horror than any other, in a certain section of the Right.

The type of Frenchman who was vaguely satisfied by the events of June 1940 has existed among us since 1814: it is privileges that create ultras. De Gaulle himself, it goes without saying, is indifferent to money. But he also holds himself above every possible and imaginable honor. From the perspective of the historical destiny that he very early in life conceived as his, a perspective that tended to identify his fortunes with those of France, what privileges could count in his eyes? By June 1940, he was faced with a dilemma that had hitherto remained buried deep within himself: he would be the first man of France, or nothing—rather, the restorer of French greatness, or nothing.

Again, it is worth noting that he has come into conflict, on the Right, with certain adversaries who are also indifferent to money, who are also disinterested men: not the "stupidest" Right, as Guy Mollet has claimed, but the Right most determined to live with its eyes closed. What these men detest in De Gaulle is his positive political intelligence. They loathe the pragmatism that makes him coldly and serenely admit the inevitable, even the loss of an empire—not by any means out of indifference, but because it is part of the situation into which the pressure of events has forced the rest of the world, and he perceives at a glance its long-run advantages and benefits. Whereas the Right I speak of pounded out the slogan "Algérie française" on its automobile horns, the De Gaulle of Brazzaville (for whom the blow was harsher than for any of us) transposed into the realm of world influence the possibilities of a France no longer a colonial power, but still an inspiration and guide, prevailing by language, culture, technology, laws. This De Gaulle has exasperated the Frenchmen hypnotized by the maps of Africa and Asia on which, in school, they colored the French possessions pink—the same Frenchmen who feel humiliated and offended by a certain underhanded move of Ben Bella's, whereas De Gaulle does not even show his feelings; he is concerned only to keep such actions from affecting the policy he has determined to pursue in French-speaking Africa. This policy is based on reason, linked to the facts imposed by history, geography, and destiny's complicity with the underdeveloped nations.

Again, this is not to say that the man who between 1939 and 1944 mustered his first forces on African soil, and by this act received the ringing proof of his legitimacy, did not suffer at the sudden and brutal rush for independence. De Gaulle may well have supposed that a French Union built around himself would resist all corrosion, but what De Gaulle suffers over his failures, what emotions he feels, do not concern the world, and he does not let the world know what they are. Decolonization belonged to the order of things, which neither he nor anyone else could halt or even limit at a certain stage.

"The fact is . . .": we must detach this common expression and give it the value of a motto. The fact having been what it was, it was up to De Gaulle not to be the trustee of a bankruptcy; had he been another man, fate would have made him into precisely that. If 1940 was not entirely a bankruptcy, if a total disaster, a shame apparently without remission, now looks to us, thanks to De Gaulle, like the starting point of a new beginning, a revival that is still going on, it is because De Gaulle has never at any moment of his life had anything of the prophet who rends his garments and calls for death about him. He has always granted events their due. He has always been able to discern what belongs to events and what proceeds from the will and power of the French people. These two factors were already distinct in his mind during the thirties, before all the cards were dealt.

In the thirties it was still within the power of the French to renounce the party regime, the Assembly governments whose impotence and paralysis in the face of a Hitler shocked the young leader and convinced him of the values of a political doctrine not conceived in the abstract. De

Gaulle is the most different man imaginable from an Abbé Siéyès in search of the best conceivable Constitution. For De Gaulle political truth is not a matter of opinion or conjecture: he has discovered it day after day. He has learned the lesson of a terrible history, and, if he has not been the only one to learn it, he has been the only one able to impose a complete transformation of their institutions upon the French.

This is what turned the entire French political generation descended from the Third Republic against De Gaulle, and what continues to turn it against him; that generation will not admit that day after day history has shown Charles de Gaulle to be right ever since 1927, and that France has revived only in so far as she has renounced a certain form of parliamentarianism. The mere presence of De Gaulle at the helm, the fact that despite the hostility of all the parties there is no power in France capable of dislodging him from it, testifies to the awareness of the French people as a whole that as long as De Gaulle is there, the parliamentary danger —a mortal one—will be averted.

In 1927, it was not because Captain de Gaulle was named De Gaulle that he became the determined adversary of the party regime. Nor was it because he detested the parliamentary system as such. But as this soldier continued to advocate the strategic and tactical switch it was still not too late to make against the threat of Nazi Germany, he grew more aware every day of the political obstacle against which his determination would be broken. Here he saw, he touched, he *knew* the irreducible contradiction between the political customs of the French and France's vocation of greatness—even her life in the most physical sense of the term. Inherited or acquired opinions played no part in his position. On the contrary, it was because no ideology influenced his thought that he became the irreconcilable adversary of a system that was leading France to her death,

and to a death within sight, so to speak: in a race to the
abyss, how could we fail to see the end? Yet what had to
be done was not being done—apparently because the general staff had adopted, once and for all, a certain defensive
concept.

Of course, during those years and until the war, and even
throughout the period of the "phony war", Colonel de
Gaulle's desperate struggle was limited to military problems. After the collapse of Poland in 1940, he addressed a
last desperate appeal to the authorities—to Premier Dala-
dier (who, it is said, did not even read it), to General Gamelin, who shrugged his shoulders. In this Memorandum of
January 26, 1940, he asserted to the eighty most important
people in the government, the High Command, and political circles: "The French people must not, at any price, yield
to the illusion that the present military immobility may be in
accord with the character of the present war. The opposite
is the truth. The internal-combustion engine endows modern means of destruction with such force, speed, and range
that the present conflict will be marked, sooner or later, by
movements, surprises, break-throughs, and pursuits the
scale and rapidity of which will infinitely exceed those of
the most lightning-like events of the past." And he specified:

The same military institutions that, on March 9, 1936, constrained us to a policy of immobility, which, during Germany's
annexation of Austria, reduced us to total inertia; which, in September 1938, and again in March 1939, forced us to abandon the
Czechs, inevitably obliged us, last September, to watch the Germans take Poland without being able to do anything but follow
the enemy's victorious advances on the map. . . . There is no
longer any active enterprise in modern warfare except that made
possible by the possession of mechanical strength. . . . No one
can reasonably doubt that if Germany, last September first, had
possessed only twice as many planes, a thousand 100-ton tanks,
three thousand 50- or 30-ton tanks, and six thousand 20- or 10-ton

tanks, she would have routed France. . . . If the enemy has not already been able to muster a mechanical force sufficient to break through our lines of defense, everything forces us to conclude that he is endeavoring to do so. . . . The defender who abides by the on-the-spot resistance of old-style weapons will be doomed to disaster. Only mechanical strength can defeat mechanical strength. The indispensable resort of modern defensive warfare is the massive counterattack of land and air squadrons. In the present conflict, as in those that have preceded it, to be inert is to be defeated. Formerly, the war of armed nations demanded the masses in combat. Today, total war demands the masses in production.

How could the author of so many prophetic pages have failed to see that the blindness and deafness of the general staff were, to a large degree, the consequence of our parliamentary mores? The ideas of the general staff were in harmony with a political regime that forbade all initiative. Behind a line of defense that was presumed inviolable and infrangible, the parties and their leaders sought to pursue their maneuvers as if nothing strange were happening in Berlin, in Rome, in Madrid—nothing that need put them on guard; as if from year to year, month to month, Hitler, too, was putting all his cards on the table . . . We will not continue the story. But strangely enough—though it did not surprise De Gaulle, for he expected as much (as we see on every other page of his *Memoirs*)—once the disaster was past, once the ascent from the abyss was begun and finally (at what cost!) achieved, it appeared that the political parties in France had learned nothing, had forgotten everything. It was unimaginable, yet it is what we have all seen: everything was to begin again, everything began again, and on January 19, 1946, De Gaulle left the helm. Not, however, without having confronted the Assembly with what, in his eyes, remained the sole problem:

I shall add a word, after having heard the balloting speeches of the spokesmen of the various groups. This word is not for the present, but already for the future. The point that separates us from some among you is a general concept of the government, and of its relations with the national representation.

We have begun to reconstruct the Republic. You will continue to do so. In whatever fashion you proceed, I believe I can say to you in all conscience—and doubtless this is the last time I shall speak in this place—I believe I can say to you in all conscience that if you proceed without taking into account the lessons of our political history of the last fifty years and, in particular, of what happened in 1940—if you fail to consider the absolute necessity for the authority, dignity, and responsibility in government—you will discover yourselves in a situation that, I warn you, will one day make you bitterly regret taking the path you have followed.

If De Gaulle has always believed in an eternal France, it is for the reasons of the heart, which in him are never separated from the reasons of reason. If nothing had changed in our institutions or in the political mores that had created the most shameful of our disasters and, should the occasion arise, would provoke still worse ones, it would have been useless for him to have chosen to become an outlaw in June 1940, to have mustered two battalions in London, to have induced England and the United States to recognize him as an ally who incarnated France; it would have been useless for him to suffer the infamy of Mers-el-Kebir and its horrible consequence—the cannonade that met him at Dakar; it would have been useless to rally around his Cross of Lorraine, in so brief a time, a great part of our empire, useless for Brazzaville to become a capital from which Fighting France spoke to the world; it would have been useless for this one man, sentenced to death by Vichy, to hold his own for four years whenever the interests of France were in question, not only against his friend Churchill, but against Franklin Roosevelt, who considered France definitely *hors de combat* and was determined to be rid of a pretentious and bothersome pseudo general (this is a combat that still subsists); it would have been useless for the

Leclerc Division to resuscitate the honor of France from
Fezzan to Paris; it would have been useless for a victorious
France, by an incredible, unhoped-for reversal, to be present on the day of the German capitulation; it would have
been useless for De Gaulle to make the miracle possible by
confronting alone, without one soldier, the anarchy of the
provinces, to succeed in integrating the French Forces of
the Interior into the Regular Army; it would have been useless for him to prevent the Americans from evacuating
Strasbourg at almost the last second.

It is amazing that De Gaulle, knowing this, should have
chosen to withdraw from the government in January 1946.
Actually, he was gambling—but not wildly. He had mea-
sured the risk. By remaining, he would have been bound,
impotent. From outside, he could act. He was not mistaken:
he acted. What this has cost us, we know. The history of the
Fourth Republic was an endless demonstration, a clinical
lesson taught on the very body of France. And the surgeon
was in the wings, ready to intervene at any moment; but
the family doctors, the general practitioners, acted as if
they preferred their patient to die; far from changing anything in the regime that was killing the patient, they carried
the demonstration to the furthest limits of grotesquerie—
but the grotesque quickly turned to tragedy.

What was De Gaulle's real intention at the time? If he
could have foreseen that he was leaving the political parties
a clear field for so many years, would he have taken the risk?
I had an interview with him then, of which I remember
little, but I find an account of it in the journal of Claude
Mauriac (at the time the general's private secretary): "My
father reported the substance of the conversation. De
Gaulle told him he was being obliged to withdraw, for the
parties had made the government impossible for him. He
realized this, and had already made his plans. The choice
of the moment was of little consequence—within a week or

so. 'It is a fact,' the general said, 'that it is impossible to govern with the parties. It is also a fact that no assembly, of whatever constitution, has ever *governed* in France, that the parliament, whatever its form, has never retained power. It is a leader the nation needs.' 'He then explained his point of view on the Constitution,' my father remarked, 'and I assure you that if he prevails, the President will have full powers.' . . . De Gaulle also explained that there had been two Resistance factions, between which no understanding was possible after the Liberation: 'Mine and yours, which was a Resistance to the enemy. And then the political Resistance, which was anti-Nazi, anti-Fascist, but in no way national.'"

I am certain that on this occasion, De Gaulle made precisely the remarks he considered likely to create the current of opinion he desired. As a matter of fact, his relative optimism was a façade. He was withdrawing only to break the threads by which the lilliputians had bound him and to create the conditions of his return "as master." Had he been able to foresee an interregnum of twelve years—and what years!—would he have run the risk?

I find it hard to understand today why I was not with him —neither at his side nor behind him—in the battle of the Rassemblement du peuple français. The chief reason came down to this, that in my eyes this so-called "mustering" of Frenchmen would muster only Frenchmen of the Right, that De Gaulle would galvanize certain national elements against the political parties, and thereby cut himself off from the Resistance Left. That I so judged matters is not what shocks me today; but my deepest thoughts were of another order, and the outcome has proved me wrong to the point where I must acknowledge the fact here. What I feared, at that moment, and perhaps what I believed, was that De Gaulle would lose, in one stroke, the mysterious power he had possessed since 1940, the power of one man confronting all the parties leagued against him—the incredible power of daring to say: "Moi, la France!" and of being believed. I was convinced that the RPF would cause him to resemble the very men he was opposing. I am accused of falling into a trance over De Gaulle; yet at that moment I was capable of losing my faith in him. Or rather, I was suddenly blinded. I no longer saw what remains the crux of his singular destiny, the element that resists every contingency and every conspiracy, the influence that makes itself felt even if De Gaulle withdraws to Colombey-les-Deux-Églises, even if, by a tacit agreement of the parties of the Right and the Left, his name is never spoken again.

After the failure of the RPF, and as the situation deteriorated, even De Gaulle's most determined adversaries found his program acceptable. For him, the only problem was to evaluate the distance between "There is still time . . ." and "Too late!"

By rereading my bloc-notes, I can name the day when I realized my mistake: there was no common denominator between De Gaulle's vocation and electoral vicissitudes. Of course I had never ceased thinking of him, turning my eyes in his direction (as the bloc-notes bear witness). But finally I, too, played the parties' game. I, too, belong to the brood of the Third Republic. Whereas De Gaulle from the first had judged the so-called "parti de la fidélité" and knew its worth, I had put my trust in the Mouvement Républicain Populaire. This decision, moreover, was convenient for me: I left it to the MRP to deal with the affairs of France and the Republic. One had one's work to think of—a literary career is never over; this lofty profession has no retirement age, and the Nobel Prize was waiting for me at the turn of the road. But I observed, I recorded the history that deteriorated from day to day until it collapsed. The first pages of the bloc-notes show that henceforth my eyes were open.

On Thursday, April 8, 1954, De Gaulle held a press conference. That day, I understood at last and confessed my sins:

Thursday, April 8, 1954. De Gaulle's press conference. It has been years since I have seen the man. He has not aged at all. As soon as he opens his mouth, one hears the same sovereign tone. His failures do not concern him. His view of France and of Europe is a simplifying one, but not simplistic. He shows the crater of the hydrogen bomb, in which no living thing can subsist, gaping before us, as Bossuet might, and in the same tone, but from this peril he derives a policy of good sense. De Gaulle, a man of the Right, has alone been able to resist the corrupt form of anti-communism that makes even the intelligent among us speak like idiots. For him, Russia is Russia. He clearly outlines a French policy opposed to the policy of abdication we have followed since his withdrawal. Greatness and misery of politics. De Gaulle consents to espouse only greatness. Which is what assures the rule of the Salesmen. In my eyes, the RPF was the absolute error. I believed that its failure would mark the end of the man who was France. Now the RPF has indeed met the fate I expected, but the man survives, and today, again, when he said, "I was France!" that past tense turned to a present in all our minds. "I shall go to the Arc de Triomphe, I shall stand alone, the people of Paris will be there, in silence . . ." No protest. What did that audience feel? It breathed the cold wind from a great altitude, from a great distance, from the time when France was *the* great nation. De Gaulle, the last Frenchman, has made us believe she is that nation still. He convinced us of it in the darkest, the most shameful hour of our history. There are still millions of Frenchmen who have not forgotten him. No one dreams of asking him: "Have you the government's consent?" This is because, by his mere presence, General de Gaulle makes the lilliputian dictatorship invisible to the naked eye. All of us left that conference with a secret, poignant regret for what might have been, for what has not been—and, I know today, for what could not be, for though greatness conceives, it is baseness that acts. The freedom we prefer to everything else ensures the rule of those who have appetites and money, in other words, power . . .

Perhaps De Gaulle realized that year that he was paralyzed: since the RPF had collapsed, the situation would
have to deteriorate still further before the parties would
recall De Gaulle—for recalling De Gaulle would mean political suicide for them.

We touch here on the dominant feature of his destiny. It
is no accident that De Gaulle has been the man of the abyss,
irresistibly summoned and virtually created by the void
that disaster creates. This is because he represented death
to all that lives by politics in France, all the professionals of
the assemblies, and one never submits to death except in
the last extremity.

Nothing is so futile as to speculate on history that has not
occurred and that might have been. Had Colonel de Gaulle
been heeded before 1939, the Army would have been
mechanized according to his views, and victory would
have changed sides. Similarly we can dream of the turn
history might have taken had the RPF prevailed and a com-
pact majority restored De Gaulle . . . But this did not happen because it could not happen. For Petain's general staff
as for Debeney's, Weygand's, or Gamelin's, and for the political fauna of the Third and Fourth Republics, De Gaulle
embodied an absolute contradiction, and at the same time
a last resort—but truly the very last. During the last agonies
of the Fourth Republic, on the eve of the first S O S sent to
Colombey-les-Deux-Églises by the desperate party leaders,
the tightrope was stretched above the void; if the man who
came forth at last, summoned by them, had been cast into
it—then that too would have been a victory for them; for although they had recalled him, De Gaulle remained their irreconcilable adversary. "Neither with you, nor without you"
is the motto that seems to be woven into the very warp of
his fate. And this is the clamp by which he has held the
world of French politics since his return to the stage. But
he has been caught in that clamp himself; he cannot save

France by his ideas without taking the French into account,
and the French manifest themselves to him in two contradictory aspects: either they are the human sea into which
De Gaulle plunges in the course of his countrywide tours,
the tide that recharges and reinvigorates him, constantly
confirming him in his providential mission, or they constitute parties and groups and cartels, which tend to dominate
the State and paralyze the executive.

As his great destiny approaches its final phase, the rules
of the game being played are simplified before our eyes. We
see it clearly at the moment I write. There is now only one
question for De Gaulle, and for each Frenchman concerned
with his own history. Once this man dies or is thrust aside,
will the institutions he has given us resist the aggressive return of the partisans of executive subordination and party
rule?

It is a question of life or death, and the proof that the nation is aware of it is that even De Gaulle's adversaries pretend to condemn the old system, swearing by all they hold
sacred that they do not want to return to it. But the Gaull-
ism-without-De Gaulle of a Gaston Defferre, for example,
awakens a mistrust on the Left that is related to the ambiguity in which the most orthodox Left itself is also
trapped, since it protests its hostility to a system and to parliamentary mores that, as everyone knows, would certainly
be reinstated and approved if Guy Mollet and his followers
prevailed.

It is the political survival of the parties that is in question.
The trump card De Gaulle holds—our card, for those of us
who are with him—consists of the French people from
whom this seigneur, this soldier, has derived his strength
since 1940, by an almost physical contact. Strangely enough,
it has taken the Gaullist experience to make a true believer
out of the dubious democrat I have been since my youth. I
had always supposed, however democratic I aspired to be,

that there is nothing so blind, so meaningless as majority rule. I discover today that if being intelligent is knowing what one wants and knowing what must be avoided in order to survive, then the majority, in France, is intelligent.

To be sure De Gaulle started from solid ground, from a rock: resistance to the occupying enemy, the maintenance of France beside her allies until victory. But in his subsequent program De Gaulle has sought neither to attract nor to seduce. At the outset, his name was not famous, like that of Napoleon III. He has never, moreover, provoked the kind of infatuation that created Boulangism. Universal suffrage, where De Gaulle is concerned, yields to no visceral, carnal impulse; on the contrary it displays a reasoned will, which all the official strata, the unions, what is called "the elite" and the press they control oppose—and it finally elects a man who does not flatter it, but who has always been in agreement with the facts and whom, at home and abroad, the facts have always proven right.

General de Gaulle's foreign policy develops as Gaullist institutions take root: they are its necessary condition. The Anglo-American hegemony is postulated on the weakness of the executive and the chronic impotence of Assembly government in France. The same reason that turns all the parties in France, Right and Left, against De Gaulle has made him the adversary whom, from the beginning, President Roosevelt sought to bypass and whom, to the end, he attempted to expel—and not only Roosevelt, but Churchill himself, despite his doubtless sincere friendship. During an interview at Marly, in 1946, De Gaulle reminded me how much England had opposed us from the very first. When I protested, "Yet Churchill . . ." "Yes," De Gaulle broke in, "in the first days . . . But he changed his mind almost immediately, corrupting Béthouart's troops whom I had converted—and acting as he did at Mers-el-Kebir, which earned

me a cannon reception at Dakar" (Unpublished journal of
Claude Mauriac).

Nothing could prevent De Gaulle, once he was in control of the government, and despite the fact that France
emerged ruined by an inexpiable shame, from restoring the
old nation to her place—the place history assigns her but
that the Anglo-Americans have never granted her, except as
a counterweight to Germany so long as Germany was powerful, and, once Germany was beaten, to Soviet Russia. To
Anglo-American minds, this place has inevitably been subordinate to the ideas and directives that in the past issued
from London and today come from Washington. All the
French parties, except the Communists, have always accepted this subordinate position; the major newspapers in
Paris and the French provinces have always, overtly or covertly, subscribed to and supported the Anglo-American
hegemony.

I have often heard General de Gaulle criticized for the
contempt in which he holds journalists. If that contempt
exists—and I have never had any direct proof of it—it must
be linked to the unshakable if masked opposition to any
French policy that, without being hostile to the United
States, seeks to be independent of that country's directives.

It is, moreover, a fact that the world is no longer caught
between two jaws as it was in 1945, and that Europe—and
France in Europe—now has freedom of movement. France,
the paralytic, has risen from her pallet.

Everything brings us back, then, to a single question, the
one asked, De Gaulle himself tells us, by "the lucid anxiety
of love." A quarter of a century of such anxiety has turned
this soldier into an intellectual obsessed by constitutional
problems, to the point where his adversaries have sought to
persuade us—and perhaps have ended up really believing
themselves—that he is no more than a politician disguised as
a general. Confronted with De Gaulle the political tactician,

General Giraud affected to be "merely" a soldier (when he was primarily a docile tool Roosevelt was using in order to eliminate De Gaulle). Later, Salan, Challe, and Jouhaud relied upon the supposed superiority over the leader of the French Resistance: that they had been commanders in combat against the enemy.

Yet Charles de Gaulle had not only been the first theoretician of a mechanized army with heavy armor, he had himself written the only glorious page of a shameful epoch on the battlefields of Laon and Abbeville: "His action, conducted on May 30 and 31 with an extraordinary brio," writes Philippe Barrès, "proved that we could indeed defeat the Germans by the same methods they employed against us. De Gaulle destroyed a great number of enemy tanks, took four hundred prisoners and much matériel, including tanks, trucks, and over sixty anti-tank cannons. Add to this the fact that on the evening of May 30, the 4th Division's advance provoked the flight in panic of a German regiment, which fell back as far as Abbeville. Night alone permitted the enemy to recover. On June 2, General Weygand gave General de Gaulle the following citation: 'Admirable leader, bold and energetic, attacked an enemy bridgehead on May 30 and 31, penetrating five kilometers into the enemy lines and capturing several hundred prisoners and an important amount of matériel.'"

Apparently De Gaulle himself has forgotten that he might, that he should, have been the Foch of World War II. Deprived of this glory, he has turned his mind to another battlefield, to another tactic in another battle: the one still in progress, whose elements were as clear to him in 1945 as they were to be ten years later, and which he still saw in the same terms. As early as the day after the Liberation, everything bearing on this point was fixed in his mind:

What particularly struck me about the regrouping parties was their passionate desire to accord themselves all the powers of the

Republic in full at the earliest opportunity, and their incapacity, which they revealed in advance, to wield them effectively. In this respect, nothing promised any sort of improvement in regard to the futile maneuvering which comprised the regime's activity before the war and which had led the country to such fearful disaster. Verbally, the politicians jealously emulated each other in denying such practices. "Revolution!" was the watchword that echoed most loudly through their speeches. But no one defined just what this meant, what effective changes were to be made in the previous situation, and particularly what authority, and endowed with what powers, would be in a position to carry them out. . . . Receiving delegations, reading newspapers, listening to speeches, I was inclined to think that for the renascent parties the revolution was not an undertaking with definite goals implying action and risk, but rather an attitude of constant dissatisfaction toward every policy, even those they had advocated themselves (*War Memoirs*, III, p. 116).

De Gaulle's adversaries, especially those who followed him up to a certain period and then were separated from him by the turn of events, accuse him of an implacable impulse to dominate at all costs. I shall not try to simplify De Gaulle. I shall not expurgate his character of all the elements in which he cannot but be steeped, like every human being. How can I question his desire to conform to a certain historical type projected into the future. Modifying Mallarmé's line about Poe, "as into himself, at last, he transforms himself," we can say that De Gaulle considers and thereby constructs himself in advance. But none of this matters—what does matter are the conditions that will make us independent of the two ominpotent allies: in De Gaulle's mind these conditions are part of the institutions he has defined and finally imposed. And if those institutions are destroyed, everything he has done since 1940 will have been useless. The game he has played for twenty-four years, which seems to have been won at the moment I write, will be won for sure only on the day when De Gaulle's successor, elected by universal suffrage, governs without any deletions having been made in the institutions of the Fifth Republic.

It was not ambition that engaged De Gaulle in events as turbid as those of May 13, 1958. It was not within his power to be recalled earlier, but the very life of the nation depended on his recall at any cost. These were the circumstances that made the return possible. If he permitted certain partisans to make use of his name for their own purposes, I shall not reshuffle the old cards of a game already played and won. Life or death hung on his return. He had to return; and who at that moment believed anything else? The instinct of self-preservation functioned even in his enemies, who were the first to recall him. De Gaulle accepts his mistakes, if he has made any, as he takes his risks. What lies within his power is leadership, and he has made his choice. Circumstances merely decide the detours that may at one moment or another alter his course, though he reestablishes it immediately.

Certain Frenchmen who are not professional politicians and do not have the reasons of a Mitterrand or a Mollet to hate him, and who are not necessarily men of the Right, oppose De Gaulle nonetheless, often with an antipathy born of the inconsistency from which even the best minds are not exempt. They are scandalized at not finding in a great man the qualities that, had he possessed them, would have made him the opposite of what he is. De Gaulle had either to break, or turn to bronze. He is not a mild man, or a tender one. Or if he is, those who know it from experience (his children, his grandchildren) do not care to tell us about it. He has passed through the fire. He has endured the baptism history reserves for certain of its chosen people.

This favorite of history differs from all others in that he has espoused the nation's misfortune; he is linked to disaster—to all disasters—not as cause but as cure. Once he takes power, or resumes it, even in the agitation of a pro-

nunciamento and a civil war, the status of France throughout the world becomes that of De Gaulle.

Thus tempered, thus forged, this man seems hard, which
does not mean that he actually is. Or perhaps he seems not
so much hard as remote; he looks elsewhere, over our heads.
He does not confuse the French with France—except in the
village squares and on the country roads. He is said to be
contemptuous of men, but what does it mean to say such a
thing? No Chief of State escapes this bitter experience: he
clashes with the political animal in man, which is a relent-
less beast whose thirst for power yields to no reasoning; this
characteristic, of course, makes *homo politicus* contemptible
in the eyes of a leader who identifies himself with France.

Granted my relish for characters, I am not sorry that this
Lillois who is so different from myself should be as destiny
has created him. Coming from Bordeaux, I have no taste for
the Midi politician, à la Fallières or Doumergue, who ruled
under the Third Republic. To all appearances, the race of
seigneurs was destroyed in our part of the country in the
twelfth century, during the Albigensian Crusade. Yet after
seven centuries, it is still a baron from the north who rules
us. I accommodate myself to the fact. Not that he does not
disappoint me at times:

> *Rien d'humain ne battait sous son épaisse armure . . .*
> Nothing human throbbed beneath his thick armor . . .

That line of Lamartine's has sometimes run through my
mind when De Gaulle failed to find the words I was waiting for: at Vercors, for example, before those survivors and
those graves . . . How cold he seemed, and how quickly he
moved on! And then I realized that De Gaulle is a man who
keeps vigil, who stares into the distance, over heads and
graves alike. He does not waste time on pity, or on mem-
ories. He does not seek to move us. The past interests him

only to the degree that he finds in it the answer he seeks for the fate that is being forged.

Yet as a Christian, one who has taken a certain position on political questions since the Spanish Civil War, and one who has never separated politics from the moral (and hence religious) law, I am embarrassed to have sided with Machiavelli, even the Machiavelli of history—who is so different from the one of legend. For ultimately the "certain way" in which De Gaulle has always thought of France is a way that has always served as a basis for her hegemony: France restored, France sovereign, France if not the mistress, at least the leader and director of Europe, and through Europe of the rest of the world outside the blocs . . . I am simplifying the "certain way," but in the long run that is indeed De Gaulle's way, and what are his means? Do they proceed from a Christian conscience? The question is apposite! We must discover whether political strategy has to derive from certain principles, or whether, nose to the ground, we need refer only to what we smell, the scent on the trail the prey has taken. For me, this contradiction implies a moral exigence in politics, which I have manifested on every occasion since the invasion of Ethiopia and the Spanish Civil War.

Still my admiration for the game De Gaulle has played since 1940 continues unabated, a game that satisfies me all the more because his means are so limited and his adversaries so powerful. Since 1940, he has never ceased to be David confronting two Goliaths. Twenty-four years after the struggle began, the weakest antagonist continues to behave as if he were the strongest, not by a miracle, nor by a grace from on high, but by an intelligent submission to what is imposed day after day. A submission and at the same time a domination, for in the long run De Gaulle submits to reality only to make himself its master.

But again, how can I accommodate myself to this as a Christian? No matter how I seek to reassure myself, I am shocked by the attraction so much skill exerts upon me. The excuse I offer lies in the pressure of events, the nature of things to which De Gaulle remains tributary. In everything he seeks the interest of France, but the fact is that today this interest is still linked to our highest, most disinterested vocation. If in fact De Gaulle's policy since 1940 has proceeded in the direction the Left desired, if De Gaulle has finally made a reality out of what seemed most difficult for the nationalistic and chauvinistic French to acknowledge, it is not because he sought to be loyal to certain principles, but because French greatness and its restoration, to which he has dedicated himself, can today be based only on the spiritual values we possess.

What would De Gaulle's policy have been had he possessed the means of greatness—those of Soviet Russia or the United States? I dare not think. But after all his genius has had to apply itself to a quite different problem: to maintain the historic place that belongs to France, which has become a second-class nation and cannot enter into competition with the great powers.

It is at this point that France's spiritual capital enters into the calculation of a realistic policy and coincides with the most disinterested views. If the Left is not grateful to De Gaulle for what he has accomplished—which should have gratified it tremendously—it is because he was not inspired by principles. We must insist upon this point. The fact that he and they share common goals has never brought De Gaulle closer to the politicians around him. During the Resistance no one could have been less alien to his supporters than this leader. But from 1944 on, De Gaulle made the Assembly aware of the basic contradiction. He informs us of it in his *Memoirs:*

As long as we celebrated, for instance, "the coming victory of justice and liberty by the defeat of fascism," or "the revolutionary mission of France," or "the solidarity of the democracies," or "the building of peace on the co-operation of peoples," the delegates were in a receptive state of mind. But once explicit dealings with the Saar Basin, the Rhine, the Ruhr, Silesia, Galicia, the Levant, or Indochina were suggested; once someone said "No!" ahead of time to what our allies would decide without us; once it was stated that if we were throwing in our lot with theirs it was not because England was a parliamentary nation, America democratic, and Russia a soviet state, but because all three were fighting against our invaders—then the members of the audience, while appearing attentive and even approving, indicated by various signs that they found the light too bright . . . (III, p. 64).

Therefore if a Christian risks nothing in following De Gaulle, it is not because De Gaulle is himself a Christian, or because the Sermon on the Mount inspires his policies. It is because the interest of France, at this moment of her history, is inseparable from her highest calling. But this, De Gaulle has, to my knowledge, nowhere explicitly acknowledged, and I wonder once again, reluctant as I am to ponder the question too long, what would have happened if De Gaulle had had the means of power . . .

On this point, the chapter of his *Memoirs* that gives most food for thought is the one describing his journey to Moscow and his meetings with Stalin. The interest here, to my mind, lies less in the facts reported (the Franco-Soviet pact, French recognition of the Lublin Committee), than in the psychology revealed. How did De Gaulle react to Stalin? Indignation, horror are not sentiments to which a statesman yields when he is dealing with a great beast of prey like Stalin. I am not surprised that De Gaulle avoided such emotions, but nowhere in his narrative do I feel that he had to resist doing so. The old wolf with the blood still on his chops interests, diverts, and on occasion impresses him. He writes, for example:

Stalin was possessed by the will to power. Accustomed by a life of machination to disguise his features as well as his inmost

soul, to dispense with illusions, pity, sincerity, to see in each man
an obstacle or a threat, he was all strategy, suspicion an ¹ stub-
bornness. The revolution, the party, the state, and the war had
offered him the occasions and the means of domination. He had
seized them, using a thorough knowledge of the complexities of
Marxist dialectic and totalitarian rigor, bringing to bear a super-
human boldness and guile, subjugating or liquidating all others.

Thenceforth, with all Russia in his hands alone, Stalin regarded
his country as more mysterious, mightier, and more durable than
any theory, any regime. He loved it, in his way. Russia herself accepted him as a czar during a terrible epoch and tolerated Bol-
shevism to turn it to her own advantage, as a weapon. To unite
the Slavs, to overcome the Germans, to expand in Asia, to gain
access to open seas—these were the dreams of Mother Russia,
these were the despot's goals. Two conditions were essential in
their realization: to make Russia into a great modern, which is to
say industrial, power, and at the right moment to bring her into a
world conflict. The first had been fulfilled, at the price of an un-
precedented expenditure of human suffering and human loss.
Stalin, when I saw him, was accomplishing the second in the
midst of graves and rubble. His fortune was to have found a people so vital and so patient that the worst servitudes did not paralyze them, a soil full of such resources that the most terrible
destruction and waste could not exhaust it, and allies without
whom he would not have conquered his adversary but who would
not have triumphed without him (III, pp. 68–69).

I sense in these last remarks an obscure nostalgia: how
small France is today! Beyond that, De Gaulle, too, seeks
to reunite those of his race—he, too, is supported, accepted
because he is necessary. He, the Knight of the West in one
aspect of his destiny, resembles this monster.

De Gaulle and Stalin are a perfect match. They speak the
same language. "If I were in your place," Stalin says to De
Gaulle, "I would not put Thorez in prison. He's a good
Frenchman . . ." And De Gaulle replies: "The French Government treats the French according to the services it
expects of them . . ." Not according to their merit, but ac-

cording to their effectiveness: this takes us a long way toward establishing one morality and thereby destroying another and introduces us to a world in which Stalin and De Gaulle, despite the gulfs that separate them, understand each other in the wink of an eye.

At the gala dinner that follows, De Gaulle watches the huntsman and the crawling, trembling pack which he alternately flogs, threatens, and caresses:

Stalin's remarks were direct and simple. He assumed the manners of a peasant of rudimentary culture, applying to the vastest problems the judgments of rough good sense. He ate heavily during each course and served himself copiously from a bottle of Crimean wine frequently replaced in front of him. But beneath these good-natured appearances, the fighter engaged in a merciless struggle was apparent. Furthermore, the Russians around the table watchful and constrained in manner, never took their eyes from him. On their part, manifest submission and apprehensiveness; on his, concentrated and vigilant authority—these were, as far as could be seen, the relations of this political and military general staff with this socially solitary leader (III, pp. 82–83).

There follows the famous page where Stalin, in a series of toasts, alternately glorifies and threatens each of these hounds who stare at him, and who tremble. Stalin always draws a laugh, but his jokes betray his ferocity. De Gaulle reports the worst of them, without comment:

"Ah these diplomats!" Stalin exclaimed. "What chatterers! There's only one way to shut them up—cut them all down with a machine gun! Bulganin! Go get me one!"

It is when Stalin jokes that he reveals himself and betrays the murky depths, the dreadful lees of his being. A little later, to make De Gaulle laugh (did De Gaulle laugh?), Stalin pretends he wants to send their interpreter to Siberia "because he knows too much." And then, the game played —and won by De Gaulle (the Franco-Soviet pact was signed

without our having recognized the Lublin Committee)—
Stalin suddenly relents, reveals himself and, incredibly, soft-
ens under De Gaulle's icy stare:

He now spoke of everything in a detached way, as if he regarded
the other men, the war, history, and himself from a pinnacle of
serenity. "After all," he said, "it is only death who wins." He
pitied Hitler, "a poor wretch who won't escape from this one." To
my invitation, "Will you come to see us in Paris?" he answered,
"How can I? I'm an old man. I'm going to die soon."

Let there be no misunderstanding: I am not trying to put
De Gaulle in the same category as Stalin. What has he in
common with that man of blood? Nothing more than being
at the head of a splendid cast in the same drama, under the
same spotlights, and at the same time. History imposes its
own morality on its performers, whoever they are, at least
during the time they are on the stage. In the wings, I have
no idea what De Gaulle is like. On the prie-dieu of his par-
ish church in Colombey-les-Deux-Églises, or perhaps at
night, at the foot of his extra-long bed, what does he say to
the Infinite Being, if indeed he says anything at all? And in
what tone does he speak? What are the prayers of Charles
de Gaulle? Does he pray? This we shall never know.

The startling thing about the portrait—Stalin as seen by
De Gaulle—is that a character out of Shakespeare breaks
free for a moment, leaves the stage, and, from the pit, observes and judges his fellow actor. I cannot share the indifference of so many who pride themselves on loving arts
and letters to whom life has offered a French hero like this
one, on the scale, at last, of a historic drama. A hero who
has, indeed, a storybook quality: as great in good as Hitler
in crime; full of calculations, certainly; capable of ruse;
nursing long grudges. But even his rancor escapes pettiness
because of the greatness that is its source and its object:
not his own greatness but that of France—and not of France

alone (as has been absurdly alleged), but of the old nation that was first among all nations, that was "la grande nation" before there was any other, and that today, resuscitated by De Gaulle, has become a kind of venerated mother of the young nations emerging from her in Africa or fertilized by her spirit in Latin America.

Such is the De Gaulle whom you hate or whom you contemptuously dismiss. Shakespeare in search of characters would have found only this one in France—aside from the supernumeraries, of course: around Coriolanus, as around Caesar's corpse, swarm the Mitterrands, the Guy Mollets, and the Tixier-Vignancours. That De Gaulle sees himself as a character out of Shakespeare and as the hero of a great history is manifest each time (and they are frequent) that he speaks of himself in the third person. General de Gaulle stands before the gaze of General de Gaulle, who observes him, judges him, admires him for being so different from all other men.

Indeed, in order to imagine how De Gaulle sees himself, any old man, however obscure in comparison with the man who concerns us, may arrive at an approximation by conducting an analogous experiment in the twilight of his life. Which of us, after sixty years of a more or less public, more or less successful or ineffectual existence, does not observe his own character as though he were watching on a screen an enlarged projection of himself in the course of a film in its last reel? The difference is that for De Gaulle the projection is not identified with an imaginary screen but with the reality of France.

That is what makes his character so singular. The pride for which De Gaulle is censured is linked to a self-veneration addressed not to himself but to what he embodies. With this man, we always return to the first sentence of his *Memoirs:* "All my life I have thought of France in a certain way"—a way that has imbued him since the first awakening of his mind, a way that has oriented all his readings, determined his admirations, made him the cadet of Saint-Cyr and later the soldier of the First World War. On that day, he offered the gift of his young life—like all the others? Yes, of course. How many other De Gaulles are dead! Those "elite" beings might have been saviors too. And by what miracle was this one spared: wounded twice in Belgium, in August 1914 and March 1915, at Mesnil-les-Hurlus. Finally, on March 2, 1916, at Douaumont, he lay wounded, unconscious after the explosion of a shell, and awakened, a prisoner.

He was alive. One man, and sometimes one woman, suffices to save a people. That is doubtless why history allows itself to squander its capital in the waste of so-called world wars, the pointless sacrifice of millions of young lives, some charged with infinite possibilities. De Gaulle was spared at Dinant, at Mesnil-les-Hurlus, at Douaumont. His incredible luck has been our own. That unknown lieutenant had to be saved in those days, so that we could be saved too, twenty-four years later.

Yet what if one of his wounds had been mortal? What other Frenchman, in 1940, would have attempted, would have dared, what De Gaulle attempted and what he dared? What other one? I cast about for a single name, and find none. That the destiny of a people is linked to a single life, to what is most fragile, most threatened, most ephemeral, is an obvious fact which both stuns the mind and keeps me from feeling much sympathy with those who have sought to strike him down.

It is a commonplace of speechmaking, a cliché of journalists to denounce the cult of personality. What is true of personality is also true of the nation: both are idols mistrusted by the conscience of the Left—and in particular the Catholic Left.

But we have learned from De Gaulle to consider only

what exists. The cult of personality? If I had to write the history of France in a dozen words, I should say: "There has always been someone at a given moment . . ." Or else: "At that moment, there was no one." The epic of De Gaulle illustrates this, as does that of Joan of Arc. And this comparison, which his enemies make a mockery, is in our eyes a matter of the obvious—so obvious that for De Gaulle's enemies there has never been any other necessity except that of striking him down, as there was no other for the English but to set up a stake, one day, in a square in Rouen.

Yes, everything has always depended on one person: those who armed Ravaillac knew this, and Charlotte Corday believed it. If Mirabeau had not died in 1789, the monarchy might have been saved. If Lieutenant de Gaulle, on March 2, 1916, instead of being wounded as he was at Douaumont, had been buried alive and his body recovered later—if he were today the Unknown Soldier under the Arc de Triomphe—the history of France would have been another history. It would have continued, all the same, because France exists, as a nation, and because she would have persevered in being one. Which brings us back to the idea of *nation* which is inseparable from that of *personality*. Personality and nation, the two so-called idols, constitute the two realities whose conjunction in De Gaulle constitutes Gaullism.

What the crowds of workers sang in my youth has not come to pass: the Internationale has not become the human race. The human race has inclined first toward a League, then toward an organization of increasingly numerous nations, increasingly defined and differentiated. The nationalist passion of the nations now coming into being in Africa was inherited from us. It is the old nation, the France the child Charles de Gaulle was already thinking about in a "certain way," that is imposing itself more and more upon a world the two atomic powers claim to dominate absolutely, with the consent and even the eager adherence of what we must indeed call the American party in France—those who in all good faith consider the Pentagon's hegemony a necessity that must not be questioned.

What De Gaulle demonstrates in the diplomatic realm, as he proved with his tanks in 1940 at Laon and at Abbeville, is that it is enough for France to have her hands free to become once again the leader of the game, even confronting two enormous powers.

De Gaulle's independence of the United States constitutes his trump card; not even hostility to the United States—it is no longer enough to depend upon America absolutely if France is to embody the hope of the world outside the blocs. By the astonishment, one might say by the stupor manifested in America because France has a policy in China and Indochina that contradicts Washington's, we can measure the distance De Gaulle has covered. The demonstration is all the more striking in that it has been made upon the debris of an empire, while everywhere, lastly in Algeria, France's colors have been struck. To have known, to have understood that what appeared to every French mind influenced by the Right, and especially to every French soldier, as a disaster and a shame, was actually a deliverance, that what seemed to be the end of everything marked the new beginning of something, something tremendous, of which we had lost even the memory—that is the honor of De Gaulle.

The fact remains that an unconditional assent to De Gaulle seems to contradict certain opinions of mine in the past. If I linger over my own particular case, it is because it concerns a whole family of minds. Indeed for a man of my generation, born and raised under the Third Republic, whose destiny as a man and a writer is framed by the two great wars, who has survived so many disasters and so many shames, one need seek no further reason for his Gaullism. It is born of the contrast between that collapse and this recovery.

But still, to the degree that as a man of letters I have been concerned with politics, especially after the invasion of Ethiopia and the Spanish Civil War, I have generally sided with the popular front and against those who are called nationalists. All my life I have been an adversary of nationalism and of Charles Maurras, whatever may be said in a recent history of the *Action française,* where I appear as an intermittent Maurrasien.

Nevertheless, it is true that between 1910 and 1925 I approved of Jacques Bainville. Indeed, my determined opposition to Maurras, which has never wavered, had nothing to do with France's foreign policy. It is the Catholic in me who, ever since his "Silloniste" eighteenth year, has sought to clarify the Maurrasien ambiguity: no, Catholicism does not espouse a certain political and social order; it need not guarantee it; it is not linked to a certain civilization; it does not constitute the patrimony of the West.

But I realize today that my determined opposition to Maurras on the religious level, which for me was essential, deflected my thought from the points where I was in agreement with his analysis. If I have so readily accommodated myself to the institutions of the Fifth Republic, it is because for forty years of my life I followed every morning in the *Action française,* as De Gaulle himself no doubt did, the implacable analysis of French parliamentary life, of its slow corruption, and of the paralysis that followed. During the period between the wars, anti-parliamentarianism in France as it was startlingly manifested on February 6* became the commonest thing in the world. France did not wake up anti-parliamentary with De Gaulle and because of De Gaulle. What must be said is that De Gaulle has continued—no

* The Stavisky riots in 1934.

longer on the blackboard, but on the crucified body of the
nation, taken down at last from the cross—the demonstration Maurras began; he has established a relation between
the political mores of the French and what happened to
them, the direct consequence of our domestic policy.

I have always considered myself an anti-parliamentarian.
But under the Third Republic, an adversary of parliament
in France did not even conceive that there might be a system for France different from the one that was killing
her, so closely did the regime seem to be identified with our
very being. It has taken the cataclysm of the war that was
lost, it has taken four years of occupation, not to destroy the
system, which survived until May 13, 1958, but to reveal
its tragic inadequacy and to make the impossible possible—
I mean constitutional reform as De Gaulle had defined it.

But if Gaullism has satisfied beyond hope the old hostility
I nursed against the parliament for over half a century, it
has also opened my eyes to a misunderstanding I had accepted for many years. Except between 1910 and 1925, I
was against nationalism—or rather against the nationalists,
whom the Dreyfus affair had forever dishonored in my
mind. Opposition to Fascism, to National Socialism became
a struggle against the deification of the nation. Despite this,
I too thought of France "in a certain way," not very different from that of Colonel de Gaulle at the time, but I did not
realize it. I was fighting in the name of a principle (Christian democracy, Christian socialism) against the racist nationalism of Berlin and Rome. The nationalism that was my
enemy concealed from me the nation to which I was bound
and whose history I tended to read only in the past tense.
As a matter of fact, I believed its destiny was over and done
with.

This was Gaullism's contribution to me: De Gaulle's Europe of patries is not opposed to Robert Schuman's Europe
in the way a superannuated and outmoded concept is op-

posed to a new idea. It simply corresponds to the facts: each nation is powerful and absolute, with its unique characteristics, passions, virtues, madness, genius—as different from any other as one human being is from another. And at the same time, Europe, too, is arduously creating itself before our eyes. It will be something different from what Robert Schuman and the "Good Europeans" of the past once dreamed of. On this level, France as a nation is brimming with possibilities which French advocates of American hegemony continue to deny, overtly or covertly. And yet in the diplomatic realm De Gaulle has demonstrated the intact power France once again possesses, and he has done so with a persuasive force increased tenfold by the fact that the maneuver was executed twenty years after the greatest disaster in our history, and during the very years that have seen the liquidation (catastrophic in Indochina and in Algeria) of our empire. That the French nation has recovered its place, regained its freedom of action, that it today polarizes the hope of the world outside the blocs, under such conditions and despite the unchallengeable position atomic weapons have given Soviet Russia and the United States—this means that Gaullism is less a doctrine than a successful experiment, a verification, a confirmation by the facts of a certain way that the child Charles de Gaulle had of thinking about France.

What then? No reservations? Have you no questions to ask? Do you harbor no doubts? Yes, and I will examine the doubt. But first let me dismiss all reproaches about the character of the man, the character that has made De Gaulle De Gaulle. I have already done as much, but I return to the point and insist upon it.

In a figure as clearly articulated as this one nothing seems to me so futile as to denounce the character that has in a sense determined his fate, or to lament the absence of the virtues opposed to the qualities that constitute his very nature: a certain mildness, benignity, bonhomie, certain possibilities of sympathy. De Gaulle has what we might call reluctant tears. His human metal has been tempered by history into a unique mold, not certainly a mold "to take or leave," for we have had to take it, willy-nilly. He who stands among the French of today who resemble him so little as though delegated to our age by the French of the old days has not offered us a choice.

Another reproach coincides with this one: the criticism of the use he has made of the Constitution, the objection to the most personal government France has ever known. On this point, it is undeniable that as long as De Gaulle controls the government, we cannot arrive at a precise idea of what the present institutions are worth. To be absolutely certain, we must wait for the election to the presidency of the Republic of a candidate of the ordinary kind. I understand why many are not resigned to this state of affairs. It is not because the consular Republic does not conflict with any of my own notions, or because it even flatters a secret predilection, that I take lightly the reactions of a certain conscience of the Left to a personal government, and to the fact that France's foreign policy is conceived by one mind, and executed according to the views and by the tactics of one man, who discusses these with no one. This is a result of the "De Gaulle Phenomenon" to which I consent with all my heart and soul, but once again I understand how others can be opposed or at least not resigned to it.

I set aside another order of objections, not because I deny their importance, but because I am incapable of a personal opinion in the matter: has France the means to implement De Gaulle's policy, or will the "inflated frog" explode in the end? I have, of course, made up my mind on this subject as on all the others, but for reasons that have nothing to do with economics. What has helped me follow the heart's reasons in a realm that concerns them so little is the conjectural character of anything in politics determined from

the economic point of view. I remember, immediately after
the thirteenth of May, at the moment of De Gaulle's accession, how Pierre Mendès-France's predictions of catastrophe
overwhelmed me, for I had no doubt that Mendès-France
was a great student of the subject; and of course he was.
To what degree he was mistaken we are realizing today.

Then have I found nothing in this regime that conflicts
with any part of myself? Am I as satisfied as I claim? Now
is the moment to reveal what I do not say but may be thinking. If I have resisted doing so hitherto, it is because, in fact,
I have always been an extreme pessimist in politics, accustomed since childhood to the worst and always expect-
ing it; and my expectation has never been disappointed.
And now, for the first time, within me the reasons of the
heart and reason itself yield to the same satisfaction.

For the first time—I repeat, for the first time—a logical
mind at grips with the situation has for twenty-four years
ceaselessly accommodated to and thereby dominated it; indeed the periods of De Gaulle's withdrawal from power
serve as a demonstration *a contrario*—of the effectiveness
of a policy? That would not be saying enough. Of a presence? Yes, of the presence of a man, a certain man, and
that man alone. It is actually against this solitude that the
democrats of the old order are mobilized, not, as we have
seen, without reason. But can I who, once again, find nothing to say against this man, or against what he has accomplished—can I approve his methods? Do I find nothing to
censure in them?

I do, indeed, have a certain objection that I do not believe
I have ever formulated. It has always been latent because it
was imprecise; and it is this objection that I must now dis-
cuss. I hesitate over what expression to give it, and what
scope. What I suffer from—no, that is not true, I do not
suffer from it!—what embarrasses me in Gaullist France is
a disproportion between the policy of greatness as General

de Gaulle conducts it abroad and the indifference to the
deterioration of the French spirit, the neglect of the youth
of France. It is as if, for De Gaulle, there were no relation
between the France he is restoring to her true place among
the nations, and the French, especially French youth, abandoned from adolescence to all the basest stimulations of
sexuality and violence. The mass media keep youth in such
a state of frenzy, one marvels that any young people escape
from it and still choose to work. I limit my reflection to the
problems raised by the young, though what we might call,
after Barrès, "the education of the soul" in fact concerns
every age, and the whole of French society reveals preoccupations and tastes that in no way correspond to the notion of greatness its leader incarnates. He himself does not
appear to be troubled by this contrast. He seems to have
dissociated once and for all the ephemeral French from
eternal France, as if he had finally decided that the nation's
greatness depends only on the mind that directs it, and that
for the rest one must trust to what the old nation still pro-
duces—despite the periodic slaughters of wartime, the hid-
eous and deliberately maintained offense of alcoholism, the
industrialized corruption of the cinema—from which the
State continues to draw each year the quota of teachers,
engineers, gendarmes, and curés necessary to make a
people.

In the totalitarian states wherever the nation's greatness
has taken a precedence over everything else; wherever a
people, at the lowest point of its history, has risen and become great—in Russia and in China—the goal has been to
make each child into a citizen. In Gaullist France, something more than civic education should be at stake. I have
often thought that the only fruitful idea we could inherit
from Vichy would be the notion of the "chantiers de la
jeunesse," the youth workshops. Under a regime where
everything ultimately rotted, there was, nevertheless, in this

area, the dawn of a success, the vestige of a direction that still marks some minds.

This reminder is enough to suggest what alienates Charles de Gaulle, a Christian in private life, from any policy influenced by a religious tenor. De Gaulle knows, as a man who knows the history of France and knows the French, what it costs to impose a moral order from outside —and what it costs religion first of all. I imagine that in his eyes grace is the affair of God Who is the God of men's hearts. Human policy seeks to interpret events, "those masters," Pascal tells us, "that God gives us from his hand," to dominate them, and to shape them for the common good. But human policy has no power over the passions except the power of supervision, a police power. How can the Christian De Gaulle forget those two marshals of France, MacMahon and Pétain? No doubt he has pondered these as two examples not to follow.

No civilian, freemason President could have avoided more diligently any interference, any pressure of a spiritual and confessional order than this Catholic general. Of course he attends, whenever it is de règle, the ceremonies of the Church, but he has never yielded to the temptation to address himself, as a member of a particular church, to the French people he leads; and at no moment has he given the impression that he could receive, much less solicit, either directives or advice from Rome.

Yet the Church, the Gallican Church, can hardly be kept out of the "certain way" in which he has thought of France. That it constitutes the very soul of France, De Gaulle believes and knows. But he does not seem to believe that the spiritual, as such, has anything to do with politics, or that it is his responsibility, as President of the Republic, to intervene directly in the shaping of young minds. Hitler and Mussolini are too close to us in time to prevent the chants of their fanaticized youth from ringing forever in our memory. Whether De Gaulle suffers, as I suffer, from a disproportion between the way in which he thinks of France, which he seeks to impose on the rest of the world, and the moral and spiritual anarchy that is everywhere manifest in France but particularly in Paris, the anarchy of which television, the radio, and the cinema have become the accomplices, we shall doubtless never know.

This great temporal leader never touches upon the spiritual. Yet it is not within his power to dissociate the two realms in reality. France's political power will be in proportion to her spiritual influence. Everything happens as if, for De Gaulle, no direct action of the political power could affect the source of that influence: the soul itself.

Doubtless this is the element of faith in this pragmatist—the element of a faith confirmed by the history of the past, the history he has survived and dominated, and the history he will continue to live through: there have always been, there will always be, in this old nation, many more than the ten just men God demanded of Abraham in order to save Sodom. Frenchmen of the race of Péguy and of the race of De Gaulle (different, in this, from Maurras and from Barrès, who predicted that the French nation would be in constant danger of annihilation if the requisites for its safety were lacking), Frenchmen like these, though they have been the contemporaries of great disasters, have never believed that France could be annihilated: even if she were dead in appearance, as in 1940, they have never doubted her resurrection. This is because there is in France a principle of eternity that manifests itself at every moment of her history and in which De Gaulle places his trust—as the helmsman, completely occupied by the maneuvers at hand, trusts the engines he does not see.

De Gaulle offers us another riddle. This man who, since 1940, has imposed upon reality the policies of the Left, and whom for this reason the Left has been obliged to support despite its suspicion and antipathy, this man who is indifferent to money and scorns wealth has accommodated himself to the capitalist system, manifesting no aversion for those who embody it, using them, and being used by them. Indeed he uses whatever the social situation gives him without passing judgment, without seeking to change anything; this is not the point on which he has received the mandate to act. It is within his power to accommodate himself to capitalism, not to modify it. Marxism has made Russia and China what they have become. Doubtless a Russian or Chinese De Gaulle (if such a thing were conceivable!) would have been a Marxist. But Marxism, at least for the present, has no place among the French données. This old people is entirely oriented toward an improved standard of living; it aspires to a certain comfort, even to a certain luxury, and first of all to its own leisure. A De Gaulle neither resents nor deplores the fact: he observes it, he takes it into account. He has not received a mission to bring a greater justice to pass on earth—at least not directly and without consulting the will of France. De Gaulle believes in the mission of France among men. His own role concerns the France he must maintain in her rank and in the place from which it will be possible for her to aid the nations.

II

WHAT WOULD De Gaulle himself think of the *certain way* in which I think of De Gaulle? We must ask him. We must confront this way of thinking with De Gaulle's words, the words he has repeated ceaselessly since June 18, 1940, addressed both to the French nation and to the rest of the world. We are not entitled to be mistaken about De Gaulle, or about the role he has assigned himself. Such an error would make us as inexcusable as Hitler's contemporaries who heard his speeches and read *Mein Kampf*.

I should therefore like to trace De Gaulle's thinking step by step as he has manifested it to us from the first day, and to reply to it, yield to it, or resist it, depending on what I feel today, hearing it again and taking into account what has come to pass and what De Gaulle did not always foresee. But he has never claimed the gift of second sight. The entire history of De Gaulle is the exorcism of historical fatality by the thought and will of one man.

First of all I want to return to the source of everything: De Gaulle's belief, his conviction that he is De Gaulle. This is not a tautology. There was once, once only in the history of the world, a man who said he was the Messiah and was not imprisoned with the mad. He was taken at his word by his friends and by his enemies; and he continues, from century to century, to be taken at his word by them. There was once, once only, a shepherdess who said the saints had

spoken to her and commanded her to deliver Orléans and
lead the dauphin to Rheims. And this she did, and paid for
it with her martyrdom. There was once another shepherdess
who said that she had seen a lady in a cave. And she, too,
was not imprisoned, and crowds from all over the world
have not ceased to touch the rock where the lady appeared
to her.

There is nothing in these three histories to satisfy a mind
that attempts to reconstruct the circumstances logically.
But it is different in De Gaulle's case. Nothing inexplicable
has occurred; he has explained even as he took action. He
has not ceased speaking and acting in broad daylight, before the eyes of the world. Let us try, then, to grasp the
mystery at its source, to discover its genesis, its birth in his
very language.

Starting from June 18, 1940, the history of De Gaulle is the
history made by De Gaulle. He no longer has a private life,
and deliberately, definitively rejects any concession, any
personal complacency. On June 19, he solemnly declared:

Faced with the confusion in the souls of the French, the dissolution of a government in the service of the enemy, the impossibility of making our own institutions function, I, General de
Gaulle, French soldier and leader, am aware that I speak in the
name of France.

Henceforth and forever, De Gaulle will take responsibility for France. "Confronting the frightening void of de-
featism, my mission seemed to me, at one glance, both clear
and terrible. At this moment, the worst in her history, it was
my duty to assume the burden of France" (*War Memoirs*,
I, p. 88). In the beginning was the act of faith. Everything
always begins with faith. But faith "with its eyes open" is
the opposite of blind faith. De Gaulle, from the first day,
sees himself, observes himself, measures himself, judges
himself. Evoking his decision of June 18, he writes:

As for me, with such a hill to climb, I was starting from nothing. Not the shadow of a force or of an organization at my side. In France, no following and no reputation. Abroad, neither credit nor standing. But this very destitution showed me my line of conduct. It was by adopting without compromise the cause of national recovery that I could acquire authority. It was by acting as the inflexible champion of the nation and of the State that I could gain the consent, even the enthusiasm of the French, and win respect and consideration from foreigners. Those who, throughout the drama, were offended by this intransigence refused to see that for me, intent as I was on withstanding countless conflicting pressures, the slightest wavering would have brought collapse. In short, limited and alone though I was, and precisely because I was so, I had to scale the heights and never again descend (*War Memoirs*, I, pp. 82–83).

De Gaulle assumed the direction of Free France only after having waited in vain for a politician or soldier more representative and more highly placed in the hierarchy than himself to arrive in London. The powers he had assumed, with the solemn promise to relinquish them once circumstances permitted, did not seem to him, initially, to require his tenure until the Liberation. He could still declare on December 28, 1940:

We proclaim that wherever Frenchmen, whatever their position, rank, or opinions, seek to resume the battle for France, we shall be with them without delay and without conditions. We proclaim that all French leaders, whatever their errors may have been, who resolve to draw the sword they have replaced in the scabbard, will find us at their side, without veto and without ambition. We proclaim that if French Africa finally rises to wage war, we shall stand by her with that part of the Empire we possess.

Without delay, without conditions, without veto, without ambition, he will withdraw: De Gaulle proclaimed it, and who could doubt it? But did he himself believe he would be led to do so? As the days after June 18 passed, the num-

ber of men capable of outranking him in prestige shrank to
the point of becoming nonexistent, except for the marshal,
who might still decide to escape to North Africa. In the military hierarchy, the provisional brigadier general already occupied a place so eminent that no one else—except the
marshal, for a few months more—could be compared to him,
a two-star general, which he will remain for the rest of his
life because he placed himself beyond the ranks, and beyond rank.

*All the French leaders, whatever their errors may have
been . . .* These few words say a great deal about General
de Gaulle's moral situation after June 1940. He was where
he was because no one else came, no one else to whom he
could hand over the command. But was there a single man
worthy of it? Those whose orders De Gaulle would have
accepted if they reached London were precisely those individuals who, by the functions they occupied, were in one
way or another responsible for the national disaster. De
Gaulle himself was not compromised by a catastrophe he
had anticipated and done everything in his power to avoid.
Thus in the nation's collapse—in which both as a citizen and
as a soldier he suffered more than anyone—De Gaulle occupied a position that enabled him to make every refusal,
every demand. In the midst of the disaster he already belonged to the future ages of honor and happiness regained,
as if he were outside time, in the service of that eternal
France for which a defeat, however grave it may appear,
can never be anything but temporary.

This explains the assurance with which he spoke, this
commander who was nothing, had nothing. By the tone of
his voice on Radio London, the few Frenchmen listening to
the exiled general about whom they knew virtually nothing
except that he had anticipated mechanized warfare realized that he was not appeasing the nation with facile con-
solations after the fact, but telling the truth when he
declared, on June 18, 1940:

Crushed today by the sheer weight of mechanized force, we can conquer in the future by an even greater mechanized force. The destiny of the world is at stake.

And they knew that he was not offering empty words when he declared, on August 12:

The French people remember that they willingly accepted the sacrifices asked by their leaders. If the French armies were surprised by mechanized warfare, it is because they were badly prepared for it, and on this matter I shall some day clarify the situation.

On July 13, he had exclaimed: "Indeed, since those whose duty it was to wield the sword of France have let it fall, broken, I have snatched up the stump of the blade." His address of August 22 demonstrated the pride of the leader who was creating rather than following events. De Gaulle *makes history,* and he has been well aware of the fact:

I say, because I see it, that our ally England grows stronger every day. I say, because I know it, that an irresistible tide is sweeping the New World to the aid of liberty. I say, because I am achieving it, that the strength of France is beginning to reawaken.

And, making history, he knew what his real situation was. In October 1940, General Catroux, coming from Cairo, joined him at Fort-Lamy. In his *War Memoirs,* De Gaulle wrote:

At the meal, I raised my glass in honor of this great leader, for whom I had always had feelings of deferential friendship. He answered, in a very noble and very simple way, that he placed himself under my orders. Éboué and all those present recognized, not without emotion, that for Catroux, De Gaulle had henceforth emerged from the ladder of rank and was invested with a duty that knew no hierarchy. No one made any mistake about the weight of example thus given. When, after determining his mission with him, I parted from General Catroux near the aircraft which was taking him back to Cairo, I felt he was departing greater than he had come (I, p. 133).

Less than a month after his June 18 appeal, De Gaulle declared, on July 13, 1940, on Radio London:

I am in a position to announce that there is already an appreciable military force under my orders, capable of fighting at any moment on land, in the air, and on the seas. Let me add that this force is increasing every day, and make known the magnificent quality of the French youth that seeks membership in our ranks. There is not a moment's doubt that this force will continue to increase with the course of the war. Frenchmen! Realize this! You still have a fighting army.

On November 29, 1940, he gave figures:

The results? Here they are! We have at this moment thirty-five thousand men under arms, twenty warships in service, a thousand aviators, sixty merchant ships on the seas, numerous armament technicians, territories in full activity in Africa, in French India and in the Pacific, important groups in all the countries of the world, growing financial resources, newspapers, radio stations, and, above all, the certainty that we are present at every moment in the mind and heart of every Frenchman in France.

The right that De Gaulle insisted upon in June 1940, a right that he owed to his lucidity and genius, was by the end of the same year no longer merely the result of his rectitude of mind, but the product of the effectiveness of his action. He acknowledged as much in his speech of December 28:

The reality is the enemy! The enemy exploiting servitude in order to demand still more servitude. The enemy pressuring the collaborators in order to demand still more collaboration. The enemy manipulating dishonor in order to impose still more dishonor.

Confronting this new collapse, we Free French have the right and the duty to speak loud and clear. We have the right, because we have never yielded to the enemy's law. We have the right, because of enemy soldiers killed or captured, because of enemy ships sunk, enemy planes shot down, by our arms. We have the right, because a thousand of our soldiers, our sailors, our aviators have died for France since the "Armistice." And we have the right, because France—betrayed, crushed, gagged—no longer speaks except by our voice.

It is noteworthy that having alluded to right and duty, De Gaulle did not return, as is his custom, to develop each of the terms, but only the former. Duty follows of itself, it was enough for him to mention it; right on the other hand was being contested.

"That part of the Empire we possess," he said on December 28, 1940. And on January 9, 1941, addressing the British:

I acknowledge, at the same time, the particular interest you are showing in that fragment of France fighting today beside its allies for the liberation of the nation and for the great common goals.

Part, fragment—these are the appropriate words. De Gaulle admitted, on the same January 9, 1941, that "Free France has literally started from nothing" but only to remind his listeners that it had "already rallied territories whose population numbers six million men" and "raised troops, launched warships, an aviation corps, a merchant fleet." On November 15, 1941, if he implicitly and retrospectively acknowledged that he had overestimated, for the sake of his cause (the cause of France), the forces at his disposal, he nevertheless continued to give them more volume than they as yet had:

Such was our goal on the first day; such it remains today, for nothing has changed. Toward this goal, we have marched without hesitating and without flagging. When it is known with what means, I believe that the world will evince some surprise. We had neither organization nor troops, neither officers nor arms, neither planes nor ships. We had no administration, no budget, no hierarchy, no rules of procedure. Few men, in France, knew us, and abroad we were only sympathetic desperadoes without past and without future.

No day has passed without our strength having grown. Everyone knows what the stages of that growth were—always harsh, sometimes cruel—but always forward. Everyone can imagine the moral and material difficulties we have had to overcome. Everyone knows the extent of the territories, the degree of military strength, the value of the influence we have contributed to the war in the service of our country. We were a dust of men. Now we are an unshakable block. We have earned the right to be proud and free Frenchmen. Above all, we have re-established in our captive people the bonds of French unity with the desire to resist for the sake of vengeance and to revive for the sake of greatness.

Thus De Gaulle hailed in the past the "handful of French refugees [who] had brought with them the eternal soul of France," without daring to say, for the present, that it was still a "dust of men." It is sometimes necessary to deceive men, or at least to indulge them, in order to save them. De Gaulle, at the start, threw dust in their eyes—or rather, in the eyes of history. What was not true became true because he said it and did it. He has always shown a preference for the expression "proceed in order that . . ." He has always proceeded in order that what he said might in fact exist.

Yet, during a London press conference after the agreement had been concluded between the United States and Admiral Robert, High Commissioner of Pétain's government in Martinique, De Gaulle, protesting the American Government's recognition of Vichy's power over the French colonies in America, used an expression to designate the true strength of Fighting France as modest as those he had used, with reference to the past, on the preceding November 15, and used it *with reference to the present:*

The representation of the French people is naturally within the French people. Being a handful of men, we cannot claim to constitute the political representation of the French people. That political representation can reappear only upon the liberation, when the French people in their sovereignty will reconstitute their political representation (May 27, 1942).

De Gaulle chose to acknowledge this weakness, doubtless because the American Government was aware of how negligible Free French material power was in the balance of forces, in order to emphasize the considerable moral weight represented by France, Fighting France.

Between this man, and the men who followed him, there was a unique and profound understanding. All who lived the epic of Free France have borne witness to it, beginning with De Gaulle himself:

The sight of the battalions, the batteries, the armored units, the completely motorized services, mingling in their ranks good soldiers of every race, led by officers who had already sacrificed everything to glory and to victory, marching past in dazzling formation beneath the blistering August sun filled me with confidence and pride. A contact was established between us, a spiritual accord that released a mutual current of joy, making the very sand beneath our feet resilient to our stride. But when the last ranks of our troops had passed, I felt this exaltation fade (*War Memoirs*, II, p. 16).

After the failure at Dakar, De Gaulle landed at Douala, where he was fervently welcomed:

This identity of nature among all those who fought beneath the Cross of Lorraine was to be, henceforth, a permanent factor in the enterprise. In every place, in every event, one could now know in advance, for all practical purposes, what the Gaullists would think and how they would behave. For example, I would meet the same enthusiastic emotion I had just encountered in all circumstances, wherever Frenchmen were present in any number. I must say that for me its result was to be a perpetual bondage. The fact of embodying for my comrades the fate of our cause, for the French multitude the symbol of its hope, and for foreigners the image of a France indomitable amid her trials, was to dictate my bearing and to impose upon the character I represented an attitude I could never again change. For me this meant, without respite, a stubborn self-supervision as well as an extremely heavy yoke (*War Memoirs,* I, pp. 130–31).

"The character I represented"—that is the phrase spoken and written by De Gaulle: the being whom he was not at the outset, perhaps, whom he became by the collective will of the French Resistance fighters who condemned him to an attitude that was henceforth to be his true nature and his true habit, to the point where a different De Gaulle is no longer imaginable.

If De Gaulle knows what his person symbolizes, he has not been unaware—even from the earliest days—of what the Frenchmen, so rare at first, then increasingly numerous, but always a minority compared to the mass of the nation, who rallied to him or recognized him represented. Hence at a meeting in Kingsway Hall, on March 1, 1941, of the "Frenchmen of Great Britain," he exclaimed in the first words of his speech:

This gathering of several thousand good Frenchmen and Frenchwomen, who have come solely because they will be together here and will share in a single emotion, is a comfort for each of us. But we must also regard it as one proof, among many others, of a fact of the greatest importance: the intensification, in the ordeal, of the national will. For France is one, France is indivisible, and we all know that what is happening in the hearts of the three thousand Frenchmen here is happening at the same time in the hearts of forty-two million others.

This text is all the more revealing in that De Gaulle was not here speaking to his comrades but to Frenchmen established in Great Britain. It was an affirmation of a reality verified first in occupied, then in liberated France, and it reveals the importance De Gaulle has attached from the first days of his action to the emotion of "being together," "sharing a single emotion."

There is the mass of Frenchmen—the mass De Gaulle embodies—that reacts in every circumstance according to the demands of national honor and national interest, but there are also the Frenchmen who lack energy, perception, disinterestedness—Frenchmen he was to find in his path, both in France and abroad, then and later. In his speech of March 1, 1941, he declared:

Some have doubted that the French spirit would resist. There has been no lack of hostile or simply frivolous men who believed that in despair our nation would suffer a kind of moral dissolution. In France itself, these men who have no faith except in their crackbrained notions, and no law except their own interest, these men whom the decadence of our regime had sustained in politics and in the army, the press, society, and business, these men rushed into servitude. Lastly, an abominable propaganda of humiliation and renunciation has managed to influence certain weak minds and certain unsteady hearts. This aggregate of malevolence, cowardice, and mediocrity may have suggested that France, damaged at the very sources of her life, would fall into the state of chronic asthenia in which nations lose the will and even the desire for independence—in short, that she would no longer be anything but a memory of the past, a victim of the present, an accessory of the future.

So much for the men of Vichy. But the men of London were not always as firm as the general would wish. He wrote in his *War Memoirs*, apropos of the pressures to which he was subjected by the British Government:

Our British partners were aided in this by the natural propensity of the French to yield to foreigners and to become divided. Among those of us who, in their careers, had dealt with foreign affairs, whether remotely or at close hand, concession was generally a habit, if not a principle. For many, a lifetime of service to a regime devoid of consistency made it virtually a principle never to say, "No." Therefore, at those moments when I was holding out against the British demands, I could see signs, even in my own circle, of astonishment, uneasiness, anxiety. I could hear people whispering behind my back and could read in their eyes the question: "What does he think he's doing?" As if it were inconceivable that one should do anything but accept. As for those French émigrés who had not rallied to us, they sided against us almost automatically. Most of them followed the inclination of their political conditioning, for which France was always in the wrong as soon as she asserted herself. And all disapproved of De Gaulle, whose firmness, which they called dictatorial, appeared to them suspect in relation to the spirit of surrender which they claimed to identify with that of the Republic! (I, p. 163.)

In a speech on May 4, 1943, De Gaulle remarked that "this dreadful and impassioned drama inspires men, men with their courage and their greatness, but also with their weaknesses and their mediocrities." What De Gaulle did not see or did not want to see after London was that the majority of "occupied" Frenchmen, even if their sympathies were with him, nonetheless remained dominated by the notion of the *two boards* on which France was gambling. Those who lost, would lose everything, both honor and life. That is what prudent Frenchmen were thinking, though by 1941, most of them were certain of an eventual English victory.

This consensus among the majority of Frenchmen De Gaulle knew by intuition and from within, just as from within and by intuition these Frenchmen acknowledged themselves Gaullists without knowing anything about General de Gaulle. But to these direct and immediate certainties he added what he learned every day from France, from the Frenchmen who arrived to enlist in his ranks or who returned from the missions he had sent them on into occupied territory. Thus he could declare, on March 1, 1941:

And what an answer our people are giving at this moment to those who doubted them! Indeed, since the capitulation, which certain hysterical leaders imposed on its stupor but not with its consent, the French nation has not for a single day lost the awareness of what it is, or the resolution to remain so. Further, in every city, every town and village, it is building the secret network of its resistance. We know what is thought, what is said, in our homes, schools, factories, markets. We know what insignia are worn over men's hearts. We know what writings circulate from hand to hand. We know what inscriptions are painted on walls. We know the meaning of the averted eyes of men and the downcast eyes of women as they pass the enemy in the street. . . . And if we needed further proofs, we would cite thousands more, as many proofs as there are volunteers who have come to join us, and against what obstacles!

But then came De Gaulle's great ordeal. In the Levant, the Free French and the men of Vichy met face to face. What De Gaulle suffered in this confrontation we can guess from this passage of an improvised address in Beirut, July 27, 1941:

And if it should happen, alas!—the last weeks have proved as much—that our effort may lead to the most painful events, I urge you to believe that no heart has been more deeply lacerated than that of the leader of the Free French. But I urge you to believe, too, that not even the greatest pain will divert us from the road we are taking to restore France to her destiny.

He repeated this in Damascus, on July 29, in these words:

Yes, the road is a cruel one; it sometimes leads to painful events, and I urge you to believe that what has transpired here during these last weeks has not found any man's heart more deeply lacerated than that of the man who speaks to you now. Yet this pain will not keep us from marching toward our goal, which is to restore France to her destiny.

That De Gaulle should ever have spoken of his "lacerated heart" will astonish those who believe that this heart of flesh is a heart of stone, those who do not realize the horror it was for a man whose essential vocation is French unity to be forced to raise one armed faction against another, even though he believed himself innocent in doing so. In these two speeches in almost the same terms (which hark back to those used on March 1), he evoked, as though to reassure himself, "what is being thought and said in all our cities and all our villages," of which he and his comrades were aware (July 27):

We know, moreover, that as we advance we are eagerly followed by the thoughts of an enormous national majority. We have a thousand sources of information as to what is being done, what is being thought in France. We know what is being said and written in our cities and our villages. We know the inscriptions being painted on our walls and the insignia secretly worn over men's hearts. We know which broadcasts are passionately listened to (July 29).

This was true. More precisely, this became proportionately true as doubt of a German victory was born and grew greater. At the start, De Gaulle had only the minority with him. But it was a minority made up of the finest (aside from those who responded only to the hatred of fascism), a minority resolved to lay down its life, which acted on that resolution. The choice history made at that moment, the judgment that weighs on the collaborators, that still marks them after twenty years, is the ultimate reason they continue to hate De Gaulle. They openly seek his death. They sigh without shame when an attempt on his life fails. They bring him, in their minds, before the tribunal of their dreams . . .

On October 2, 1941, De Gaulle broadcast this information from London:

The same sentiments and the same will that inspire the Free French and that have allowed them to return to the war for liberation with an important part of the Empire, a considerable military, naval and air force and a notable spiritual and moral influence, these same sentiments and this same will are appearing today in the enormous majority of Frenchmen. A permanent correspondence has been established between the thoughts and desires of our compatriots in Paris, Lyons, Marseilles, Lille, Rennes, or Strasbourg and the thoughts and desires of those in Brazzaville, Beirut, Damascus, Nouméa, London, or New York. A vast

French resistance is gradually re-forming, which we have every reason to believe will have an increasing influence on the events of the war and which, on the day of the Allies' final triumph, will grant French democracy, renewed by its ordeals, a place in the victory.

Let us note (we shall have many occasions to return to it) the allusion, at this early date, to a renewed democracy. Sometimes, when De Gaulle recalls or celebrates the abnegation of his companions, it is his own labor, his most personal sacrifices that he evokes, quite secretly and in a manner all the more moving thereby. Thus in a speech of November 15, 1941:

What are we? Nothing is easier than to reply to this question. It will be seventeen months ago tomorrow that it was first raised and answered. We are Frenchmen of every origin, condition, and opinion, who have decided to unite in the struggle for our country. All of us have done so voluntarily, purely, simply. I shall not be so indelicate as to insist on how much suffering, how much sacrifice such a decision represents. Each of us is alone in knowing, in the secrecy of his heart, what it has cost him. But it is from such an abnegation as well as from such a coherence that we derive our strength.

Here, once again, is that heart of De Gaulle's which so many Frenchmen claim they have never heard beating. "The secrecy of his heart . . ." It is with a feeling of both reticence and tenderness that I quote this swift acknowledgment of the price that must be paid for so much glory. De Gaulle himself will not readily mention it again after the Liberation and the turning over of a new leaf. But in London he did not forget it, did not underestimate it. On April 1, 1942, speaking not to his compatriots but to the British, De Gaulle evoked, in passing, "the instinctive and somewhat legendary mystique that sustains those Frenchmen who, without laws, without rights, without government, brave death on the battlefields or before firing squads, expose their families to reprisals, renounce everything they possess." These "French citizens committed to suffering, death, and passion in the Resistance," De Gaulle explained to his allies, in case they had not understood, "are in the service of no one except France." The laconic tone of these few words: *without laws, without rights, without government,* reveals what De Gaulle himself was suffering. We can never fully realize what the June 18 act of disobedience could mean to a man who set the State so high.

If we must further convince those who accuse De Gaulle of being heartless, this is the moment to repeat the cry this man of stone could not restrain when, in his *War Memoirs,* he came to the epic of Bir Hakeim (June 1942):

I thanked the messenger, told him he could go, shut the door. I was alone. O heart throbbing with emotion, sobs of pride, tears of joy! (I, p. 298.)

This is close to the accents of a Pascal. But what accents of France has De Gaulle not made his own? All are his, though he is not the master of all equally: the moralists suit him better than the Romantics and, among the latter, Chateaubriand inspires him more than Barrès.

Sometimes what he confessed (long after the fact) in his *Memoirs,* permits us to verify the impression his public pronouncements made. Thus we suspected we had discovered a half-confidence—and how moving it was!—in his famous Albert Hall speech of June 18, 1942, notably in this passage:

And certainly when two years ago we flung ourselves desperately—there is no other word—into the fulfillment of our national mission, we were obliged to take, in total darkness, three steps that were no less than acts of faith . . .

The anguish he that day acknowledged for the past, and for the past alone, remained apparent to us in that present when he declared it to be behind him. This present in its turn became the past about which he could henceforth speak more frankly at the moment when he ended (and with what intensity!) the first volume of his *War Memoirs* —confirming what we had divined in rereading the Albert Hall speech where he felt "the soaring of joy":

The acclamations fall silent. The meeting is over. Each person returns to his task. There I am, alone, face to face with myself. For that confrontation, it will not do to adopt an attitude, or to cherish illusions. I draw up the balance sheet of the past. It is favorable, but cruel. "Man by man, bit by bit," Fighting France has assuredly grown solid and coherent. But how many losses, sorrows, agonies have been required to pay for this result! . . . And I, poor man that I am, shall I have the clear-sightedness, firmness, and skill to master these ordeals all the way to the end? Even if, indeed, I contrive to lead to victory a people at last united, what will be its future then? How many ruins will in the meantime have been added to its ruins, and divisions to its divisions? At that moment, with the danger passed and the illuminations extinguished, what waves of mud will break over France?

A truce to doubts! Poring over the gulf into which the country has fallen, I am her son, calling her, holding the light for her, showing her the way to rescue. Many have joined me already. Others will come, I am sure! I can hear France now, answering me. In the depths of the abyss, she is rising up again, she is on the march, she is climbing the slope. Ah! mother, such as we are, we are here to serve you (I, pp. 301–2).

He hears, yes, he will never stop hearing *France answer him.* Here the great majestic tone is both that of Bossuet and that of Chateaubriand. De Gaulle raises his pitch to the limits of two styles. He is inspired by both. And the passion his exclamation reveals helps us discover the difference between the political and racist nationalism of the Right under the Third Republic and this love beyond all class interest, all ideology—this reasonable and reasoned love which knows that the heart of Europe beats in Paris and that the mind of Europe is defined there.

In his declaration of March 14, 1943, in reply to the assurances given in Algiers by General Giraud "as to French sovereignty, respect for the laws of the Republic, and the condemnation of Vichy," De Gaulle, referring to "the doctrine of Fighting France," repeated: "The countless instances of faith that reach us from France prove that this doctrine is passionately approved by the enormous majority of the oppressed nation." And on May 4, when nothing had yet managed to convince General Giraud and those who set him against De Gaulle:

If we have chosen today to celebrate the latest arrival of our comrades from France, it is . . . because in their persons we hail the most recent witnesses of the indissoluble union established once and for all between the Fighting French and the mass of captive Frenchmen.

If we needed proof that the road we have followed for what will soon be three years, without a single detour and without a single hesitation, is indeed the road that national instinct has acknowledged as the way to salvation, the presence of these good Frenchmen who have reached us against the worst obstacles would suffice to give us a comforting certainty.

And when we listen to them, coming as they do from every part of the national territory, representing all the diverse conditions, all the diverse opinions of our people, and they tell us in the same voice and with the same enthusiasm that everywhere, in every milieu, the immense mass of Frenchmen, in their misery and their struggle, has morally rallied around Fighting France, we feel inspired with marvelous confidence, we feel more resolved than ever to march ahead.

After his first visit to a fragment of liberated French territory, De Gaulle, reminding the members of the Consultative Assembly of Algiers on June 26, 1944, that if France was not yet officially recognized by certain allied governments as a belligerent power among the United Nations, at least her arms were now recognized, added:

We choose to see, in the particular agreement I have just mentioned, a favorable augury for those still to be concluded. We believe moreover that each passing day brings a new confirmation of what is merely common sense. In any case, the Assembly will permit me to emphasize that the tremendous national fervor which the President of the Government has recently observed among the populations of the liberated fragment of Normandy, a fervor that he interpreted as giving him a sacred obligation toward the nation and toward the Republic—this national fervor affords a further argument. If it has been encountered in the hundredth part of the liberated metropolitan territory, who can doubt that it will be encountered identically in the other ninety-nine parts? Gentlemen, this fervor can only confirm us in our duty to demonstrate and assert all that is due to France, in our concern to redouble our efforts in contributing, with all the strength we have, to the defeat of a hated enemy, at the side of our valiant and cherished allies.

Contrary to custom, I have not taken this text from the Berger-Levrault edition of De Gaulle's *Discours et Messages* (1946), the only definitive edition approved by the general, but from the Égloff edition (1945). De Gaulle has always written his speeches with the greatest care. We read, for example, in his *War Memoirs* when he is describing his private life in Algiers: "At 'Oliviers', in the evening, I isolate myself to work on my speeches, which are a constant burden to me" (II, p. 173). The same passage from his speech of June 26, 1944, not as recorded by the stenographer, but as written and corrected by De Gaulle, is shorter. It should be noted, however, that such differences between published texts are relatively rare. They are found only in improvised speeches or in certain parliamentary addresses.

In Bayeux, on June 15, 1944, revisiting the soil of France for the first time since June 1940, De Gaulle had said:

We are all moved at finding ourselves together again in one of the first cities to be liberated in metropolitan France, but this is not the moment to speak of emotion. What the nation expects of you behind the front is that you will continue the battle today, as you have never ceased to wage it since the beginning of the war and since June 1940. Our cry now, as always, is a battle cry, for the road of battle is also the road of freedom and the road of honor.

In liberated Paris, on August 25, 1944, this, according to one of the published versions is how General de Gaulle began his speech at the Hotel de Ville: "Why should we all conceal our emotion?" Yes, why? Who thought of doing so, in that overwhelmed crowd, except De Gaulle himself? For this text, perhaps transcribed from broadcasts or inaccurately reproduced by the reporters, De Gaulle has substituted another, more elaborate one, in which we recognize a more characteristic tone. It begins nevertheless as follows:

Why should we conceal the emotion that seizes us all, men and women alike, as we stand here, in our Paris liberated by its own hands? No! We shall not conceal this profound and sacred emotion. There are moments that transcend each of our poor individual lives.

In his *War Memoirs,* recalling the success of a "meeting so long dreamed of, and costing so many efforts, disappointments, and deaths," De Gaulle evoked the occasion with a tremor he did not attempt to analyze. But his first reflex at such a moment, on such a day, had been, as it was at Bayeux the preceding June 15, to conceal his emotion instead of giving himself up to it. Yet was it not, as I have already noted, the same emotion that was felt, during those first days of the Liberation, by those who so joyously, so apprehensively saw him for the first time?

He has further written in his *Memoirs,* apropos of the glorious progress down the Champs-Élysées on August 26, 1944:

It is true, finally, that I myself have neither the physique nor the taste for those attitudes and gestures which can charm the public. But I am sure they are not expected of me (II, pp. 349–50).

They are expected; France expects them still—as De Gaulle knows, though he does not care for them. The combat was not over with the liberation of Paris; nor would it be over with the war. There was no question of relaxing, for the effort had to be continued for a long time. Yet beyond such immediate disappointments, there was the "contact," the "spiritual agreement," the "France that answers him," the communion that he experienced first with the Free French, then with the French people, and that he will ultimately, he seems to believe, experience with the French of yesterday, today, tomorrow, and eternity.

De Gaulle dates a great number of his public appearances after June 1940 in terms of history, and also of his personal history—the two are no longer separate. Seven days, nine days, seventeen months, two years . . . Thus he counts the days, the months, the years, until that November 17, 1945, when he declared himself ready to "entrust to another the task of directing the affairs of the nation" and to put down, "without bitterness, the burden that I did my best to carry for five years and five months during the most perilous years of French history."

Strange, this mania for chronology in a man who places himself outside time, facing an Eternal France, but it is more comprehensible when we realize that he is counting, from June 18, 1940, the years of a reign that even his long withdrawal from public life does not seem to have interrupted in his eyes. He knows that he continues "to belong to the nation," even and especially if he no longer governs it:

This settled, we retired from the scene, not only in order to prevent what, by virtue of events, we symbolize (which belongs to the nation as a whole) from becoming embroiled in party strife, but also so that no bias about any one man who was head of the state, could prejudice the work of the legislators (Bayeux, June 16, 1946).

And if, sometimes, De Gaulle describes himself with apparent humility as just another Frenchman, merely having more responsibility than the rest, it is only to make more evident what he truly represents:

Such should be the object of the Constitution of the Fourth Republic. By saying as much, I am expressing the opinion and the sentiment of a Frenchman whom the gravest events have placed in a position to measure the conditions of salvation and of the conduct of the State, and who solicits no mandate, no function, no position (Declaration of August 27, 1946).

Addressing the French people on the eve of a referendum in which this Constitution, which he rightly judged to be a poor one, risked being (and was to be, in fact) adopted, De Gaulle exclaimed:

These are our convictions. They have no party. They are of neither the Left nor the Right. They have but one object, which is to serve the nation. This is acknowledged by all the men and women whose hearts and minds we have often had the honor and the comfort of touching when we appealed to them to join us in order to serve France (Épinal, September 29, 1946).

When *this ultimately united people*, whom he had led to victory, divided against itself immediately afterward, De Gaulle attempted a rassemblement, literally a re-assembling, a union, the Rassemblement du peuple français which, as I said at the time, seemed to me an "absolute error" (a judgment with which I no longer agree, as I have already indicated above, and to which I shall have occasion to return). And then came the press conference of April 7, 1954, where I heard the general say that astounding sentence: "J'étais la France"—I was France—and felt, as I have remarked, that the past tense became, for us, a present. No doubt it had never ceased being one for him, since to the question: "This year, the official ceremonies for the tenth anniversary of the Liberation will be organized; what part do you plan to take in them?" he replied:

The Liberation has taken place, and that, of course, is the important thing. Now come the anniversaries. They are for everyone. I have been told that this year they will be celebrated under the highest official auspices. I have no objection to that. But if this be the case, how should I, who have no official status, figure in those ceremonies?

However, aside from the ceremonies thus anticipated, I believe I shall, this year, participate publicly in memory of our griefs and our glories. This is how I shall do so.

On Sunday, May 9, the date of the day following the victory in which I had the honor to lead France, the State, and the Armies, and the feast day of Joan of Arc, I shall go to the Arc de Triomphe. I have not been there since November 11, 1945. I shall arrive alone and without escort at four in the afternoon. Under the arch, I shall stand alone to salute the Unknown Soldier. Then I shall leave alone.

I ask the people of Paris to be there to show that they remember what was done to save the independence of France and that they intend to preserve that independence. I ask the veterans of both wars and of Indochina to surround the monument. The garrison of Paris will perform the necessary honors and trumpet calls. The splendid police of Paris will see to the maintenance of order, access to the ceremony, and traffic. All of us who are present will not say a single word, not utter a single cry. Above the communion of this tremendous silence will hover the soul of the Nation.

Thus the man who, officially, had no vestige of power gave orders to the public agencies, even specifying the details of what the duty of the police would be, without its occurring to anyone, in the nation and even in the government, to protest. Not even to express surprise. The general, in his retirement, possessed a power that he would employ at the opportune moment. Since the RPF did not constitute the electoral majority that would have allowed De Gaulle to effect the revolution that could not be postponed indefinitely, years earlier and in an orderly fashion, the general kept silent, kept watch, waiting to be called, praying, no doubt, before the spectacle of national degradation, that the call would not come too late. Then came the events of May 1958. On May 19, this is how he ended his press conference at the Palais d'Orsay: "Now I shall return to my village and there will remain at the disposition of the nation." Then there passed, between him and ourselves, something that we were to experience once again when, writing to M. Vincent Auriol, he envisaged the possibility that his return to power would be blocked:

In that case, those who, by a sectarianism I find incomprehensible, will have prevented me from once again saving the Republic when there was still time will bear a heavy responsibility. As for myself, I shall have nothing more to do, until my death, than to sustain my grief.

On September 26, 1958, two days before the referendum, De Gaulle terminated his televised speech thus:

By asking you to choose the State's effectiveness and national unity, I believe I am expressing what so many generations, who have built the nation down through the centuries, have desired for it. I believe I am saying aloud what in their hearts all Frenchmen desire for their country, even those who, for private reasons or passions, will yield to the negative. I believe I am answering in advance for the idea of the nation that will be held by our children and our children's children.

To each and every one of you, I entrust the fate of France.

Thus he had the certainty of acting, *also*, in the name and with the consent of his opponents! On October 23, he declared at the opening of his press conference in the Hotel Matignon:

All those who voted "Yes"—and there were many—voted joyously, and among those who voted "No," how many did so reluctantly!

De Gaulle had assumed responsibility for France to the point where he believed that he was satisfying even those Frenchmen who had refused him their mandate.

After his election to the presidency of the Republic on December 21, 1958, by 78 per cent of the vote, he declared on December 28:

Above all, Frenchmen, Frenchwomen, I want to tell you that I accept the mandate you have entrusted me with. Your decision was indicated during the national crisis last May, confirmed by the referendum, repeated by the elections, and emphasized by the vote of the electors last Sunday.

The national task that has been incumbent upon me for eighteen years is thereby confirmed. As guide of France and head of the republican State, I shall exercise supreme power in what is henceforth its full extent and according to the new spirit that has granted it to me.

A surprising affirmation on the part of a man who had not been in power for nearly thirteen years. He did not quite say that for eighteen years there had been no one between France and himself, but rather that he had not ceased during all those years, even when he was out of the government, to feel responsible for France.

During the episode of the Barricades, De Gaulle appeared in uniform on television on January 29, 1960—and on the verge of prevailing once again, he once again concluded his address thus:

Lastly I speak to France. Now, my beloved old country, we are together once again confronting a terrible ordeal.

By virtue of the mandate given me by the people, and by virtue of the national legitimacy that I have embodied for twenty years, I ask all my countrymen to support me, whatever the eventuality.

For twenty years, he had been France. He said so quite simply. Who doubted the fact?

All who heard De Gaulle exclaim, in those agonizing hours: "Now, my beloved old country, we are together once again, confronting a terrible ordeal," and who were moved by the words, knew that the general, though he minimized the new danger the nation had incurred, was telling the

truth when he said, at the end of February 1960, on his
way through Lodève:

> This unity was manifested quite recently in a circumstance
> that was not very dramatic, but that might have become very
> serious; we felt, from one end of the country to the other, a single
> heart beating, a single will made known . . .

That heart was the nation's, which beats in the same
rhythm as his own, to the point where he is conscious of
feeling and acting for that nation, not only of representing
it but of unifying it in himself. In Chambéry, early in October 1960, he could repeat:

> I have no other raison d'être, as you know, than this unity. I
> am in a sense its symbol and its guarantee: events themselves
> have brought this to pass. This is the service I can render during
> the days that are left to me, which are numbered.

On January 6, 1961, before the referendum of the eighth
when De Gaulle asked the French people to approve Algerian self-determination, to allow the Algerian population,
once peace was established, to choose its own destiny, the
general again spoke directly to the nation, as is his habit:

> Frenchmen, Frenchwomen, you know that it is to me that you
> will be answering. For over twenty years, events have brought it
> to pass that I have served as a guide to the nation in the grave
> crises that we have survived. And now, once again, my duty and
> my function have led me to choose our path. Since it is a harsh
> one, I must, in order to follow it to the end, have national support,
> in other words, a majority that is in proportion to the goal. But
> also, I need—yes, I need!—to know what is going on in your minds
> and your hearts. That is why I turn to you, over the heads of any
> and all intermediaries. In truth—as everyone knows—the matter
> is between each of you and myself.

This direct contact with the people is the great novelty
first radio and then, to a still greater degree, television have
made possible.

During the April 1961 putsch, when De Gaulle, equal as always to the situation, concluded his message: "Frenchmen, Frenchwomen! Help me!", we felt in total communion with him, stirred to our very depths. (This expression, which came spontaneously to my pen, was used by De Gaulle himself, I realize, when he said, during the events of May 1958: "In the past, the nation, stirred to its depths, has entrusted me with the task of leading it to salvation . . .")

In March 1962, addressing the nation *directly* on two occasions, De Gaulle asked for its *direct* approval. On March 18, he reminded the nation that the signing of the "cease-fire" in Algeria, the arrangements for self-determination there, the prospect of an independent Algeria closely cooperating with us, satisfied *the reason of France.* And he added:

But above all, what is done to rescue the possibilities of a fruitful future from a deplorable struggle will be due to the French people. For it is the French people who, thanks to their good sense, solidity, and the confidence they have constantly given to the man who bears the burden of leading the State and the nation, have permitted the solution to develop, and to reach its conclusion. I say this not, believe me, out of national boastfulness or political demagoguery. I say it so that our nation may stand fast in the consciousness of its own worth.

Frenchmen, Frenchwomen, in order to ratify formally what has been decided, in order to do what must be done, in spite and because of the final obstacles, there must now be a clear expression of national approval and confidence, which means: your own. I therefore intend to ask this of you.

And on March 26, De Gaulle submitted to the French people the projected referendum bill, proposing formal adoption of "the measures provided for by the governmental declarations of March 19 concerning, on the one hand, cease-fire and self-determination in Algeria, and on the other the association of France with that nation if, as everyone believes, it chooses to become independent":

Further, the President of the Republic must have the means to apply these measures; I therefore ask the nation to approve my taking them. The matter is of such importance that it requires the sovereign agreement of the nation in a direct fashion. . . . Lastly —I can and I must say—a strong and affirmative answer, which is what I seek, to the question I am putting to the French is, for them, an answer to me personally that they give me their adherence in my function as chief of State; that they grant me the right to do what must be done to achieve our ends, despite all obstacles; in short, that in the arduous task which lies ahead of me, and of which the Algerian question is but one episode among others, I have their confidence today and tomorrow as well.

Frenchmen, Frenchwomen! You see the issue. The vote of "Yes!" I ask each and every one of you to give will weigh heavily upon us all!

By saying, "is an answer to me personally," De Gaulle again emphasized the personal link that exists between the French and himself. If he speaks as a leader, it is less, apparently, as the President of the Republic than as "General de Gaulle," an embodied entity, the nation's guide since 1940, even when he no longer occupied an official position. The beginning of one of his improvised—and consequently less guarded—speeches, made at Chaumont-sur-Marne on April 26, 1963, is significant in this respect:

You are aware that so magnificent an assembly cannot fail to touch the heart of the President of the French Republic, especially because he is General de Gaulle.

Let us repeat: as he has renewed and legitimized the concept of the nation, as the nation has again become, for him, reality, soil, flesh and blood, as well as mind and soul —in a word, a person among the other persons (the other nations) who constitute Europe, it has come to pass, by the will of God or of history, that this person, France, has for twenty-four years been embodied in one man, and this man is De Gaulle, and it is not within the power of either his enemies or his friends to alter the case.

During his many trips in the French provinces, De Gaulle —and he has been censured for this—has repeated the same speech in each region, in each city, changing only the name of the département and the city. But if he flatters the local pride of the inhabitants, the general is not dissimulating about the sentiments they inspire in him. It is not, of course, as citizens of Quercy, as Limousins, or Jurassiens, that his hearers interest him. But they participate as Frenchmen in what he loves most in the world, what he has given most to and what he expects and receives most from. When they are reread in this spirit, the end of any of his improvised speeches no longer appears to be a peroration suited to the occasion. For example, his declaration in Cahors, on May 17, 1962:

I have often said to the French: "Help me!" A man is a man, and setbacks are setbacks, wherever he may be, whatever the rank he may occupy; disappointments are disappointments; difficulties are difficulties. But France is France, and must be served. This morning, I repeat, you have helped me do so. I thank you for it with all my heart.

In Limoges, on May 20, 1962:

Thank you, in particular, for giving me one more reason to be certain of France's destiny, notably by offering me the sight throughout the Limousin and here, today, of your magnificent young people, who are the hope of the nation. Let all the young men and women here remember that on May 20, 1962, De Gaulle stood before them and told them: "You will be responsible for France, and we have confidence in you."

In Lons-le-Saunier, the following month:

Today, June 15, they have seen and heard De Gaulle. . . . If they remember this, my trip and my appearance here will have served a purpose. And a purpose for me as well, for I carry away from this magnificent meeting a comfort which is and will be precious to me. When one bears certain responsibilities, as I have said before and I repeat it here, nothing is more useful, nothing is more encouraging than this direct contact, this direct understanding, which I have experienced with all of you this evening.

A *direct contact* which is, as in the days of Free France, a contact of souls. De Gaulle, in his solitude, has a physical need for such contact, which explains, far better than any ulterior motive of getting votes, his fondness for making trips through France. This Antaeus draws his strength from the living soil, which he must touch.

And if he speaks first of all to the young, this is not part of the demagoguery that is so widespread today, but a moving effort of the "old man he now is" to communicate, through them and through the witness they will bear, with a time when he will no longer be here to serve France and to speak in her name. Several of the speeches made during his journeys conclude with the same exclamation: "You have seen General de Gaulle, and he has told you of his certainty of France's great destiny." The young people of Digne heard him one day in October 1960; those of Toulon on November 8, 1961. The young people of Charleville were to hear him on April 22, 1963; those of Châlons-sur-Marne, Épernay, and Troyes in the days to follow. And he would say once again in Rochefort, on June 13, 1963:

All the young people here listening to me, all the young people who will doubtless remember having heard General de Gaulle say in Rochefort that he has confidence in France's destiny, provided her children remain united to serve her—now, in their turn, will assume the nation's responsibilities, will know from generation to generation what has to be done.

We must have the courage to confess that the young are not attracted to De Gaulle. The young are attracted to those who flatter them, who satisfy their desires for violence. Some young men are fascists by instinct. A coldly reasoned and calculated policy is not their strong point. In Algeria, De Gaulle abandoned the shadow for the substance: a thing these young men were least likely to understand. Yet what does this turbulent mob, which tomorrow will be swallowed up by another tide, matter? De Gaulle rises above such eddies: it is not from the young that he derives his strength, as Hitler did, but from the whole people, from its women as much as from its men, and from the old as much as from the adolescent. His goal is to preserve France by the support of all, by the institutions that he has given France and that will save her, if she keeps them.

I T IS what he already sees that enables De Gaulle to foresee. It is what he knows that sustains what he does. That is, of course, within the bounds of his possibilities, which were almost non-existent before 1940; still limited long afterward; then, after January 1946, again reduced to advice and reproach, although these now benefited from the prestige of the man who offered them. When he is unable to take action himself, he says again and again what action must be taken: what France did not do, and what Germany achieved (the creation of a mechanized force); what the politicians refused to do and what political reality demanded (constitutional reform). If De Gaulle prophesies, it is his intelligence, his genius, that allow him to discern, in the tangle of the present, the threads out of which the future will be woven. For this commonplace image (the kind he himself never hesitates to use) we might substitute another, quite as unoriginal but just as exact—for a quarter of a century, De Gaulle has tirelessly hammered in the same nails again and again, repeated the same ideas, in the hope— ultimately rewarded, at least in the constitutional realm— of translating them into facts.

If his goal in London, in 1940, was to bring France back into the war, it was also to organize the government provisionally entitled to control the policy of Free France, which was France herself. In the Manifesto broadcast from Brazzaville on October 27, 1940, in which he acknowledged that "a legitimate French government no longer exists . . . the organization located in Vichy which claims to bear this name [being] unconstitutional and subject to the invader," De Gaulle stated:

It is essential, then, that a new government assume the responsibility of directing the French war effort. Events have imposed this sacred duty upon me. I shall not fail it.

I shall exercise my powers in the name of France, and solely in her defense, and I take a solemn oath to account for my actions to the representatives of the French people, as soon as it is possible for that people to designate those representatives freely.

One of the "elements that constitute the basis of the Free French movement . . . is the refusal to recognize as valid the authority of a government that is irregular from the constitutional point of view and, further, placed in a position of dependence on the enemy." Thus De Gaulle on January 9, 1941, again emphasized the to him unconstitutional character of the Vichy Government. He continued:

The awareness the Free French have of what they already represent, and what they will represent tomorrow, merely confirms them in their resolve to be nothing but the servants of their nation. Doubtless the nation's dreadful situation and the necessities of war will oblige them to make decisions and take actions outside the normal context of government, since that context has been destroyed. . . . But the Free French will usurp no function. It is not they who are destroying rights and liberties under the pretext of effecting a supposed national revolution to set up a European order whose rules will be dictated by the enemy. They declare that it is the responsibility of France, and France alone, to determine, when she can do so, her own regime and her own institutions. They proclaim that when there is again a regular French government, independent of the enemy, and a true national representation, they will accept the orders of their legitimate government.

After the German withdrawal—and after final victory—he was to say of Vichy, more subtly, in Bayeux, on June 16, 1946:

Wherever the Cross of Lorraine appeared, the scaffolding of an authority that, though apparently founded on the Constitution, was only ephemeral crumbled.

And in Vichy itself, in 1959:

Now, I am going to tell you a confidence that you must not repeat: I am obliged to admit that I feel a certain emotion in being in Vichy officially. You understand the reasons. But whatever our differences have been, our history is one history, we are one people, the one, the great, the only French people. It is in Vichy that I say this and that I have wanted to say this to you. So much for the past.

And I ask myself: why was De Gaulle so moved in Vichy? Was he troubled? No, not troubled. What he had done, he believed he had to do. And yet—say what you will, the Vichy Government, founded by a delegation of the National Assembly with the quasi-unanimous consent of the nation and recognized by the ambassadors of the entire world, including the United States of America and the papal nuncio, was legal. Its legitimacy was an opinion and debatable, but not its legality, not at least until Germany invaded the Unoccupied Zone. I can see some excuse for confusing the Frenchmen who put their trust in Marshal Pétain, the universally recognized legal head of State, with those who deliberately served the enemy and betrayed their brothers. The policy of collaboration with the occupying Germans inevitably led to this ambiguity. For a Laval or a Brinon not to figure as traitors, Germany would have had to win the war, or at least not lose it. De Gaulle knew from the first day that Germany would lose the war, but Laval perhaps believed in the supreme weapons toward which Hitler extended his trembling hand during the last minutes. De Gaulle could lose. There was a possibility that he *might* lose. However weak it was, it gave an excuse to those who were playing the other card. And that they be punished for being mistaken is the law in politics: error is crime. But not punished with death and not dishonored. That is what I have believed and said from the first day—and what I still believe. The legitimacy of General de Gaulle, which history has consecrated, does not destroy the legality of Vichy. But De Gaulle answered me in advance, on January 9, 1941, in a speech made in London:

The men who have seized power by a pronunciamento of panic, the men who in a single day have destroyed the nation's institutions, suppressed any representation of the people, forbidden the expression of public opinion by any means, the men who have accepted not only servitude but collaboration with the enemy, to these men Free France grants neither justification nor legitimate power. Free France opposes their political authority by the whole tradition of French liberties, and unless they return to their duty, that is, to the war, Free France contests their military authority with this remark of Napoleon's: "A general who has surrendered to the enemy no longer has the power to give orders."

On September 23, 1941, De Gaulle, receiving the representatives of the press, announced the creation of a National Committee of Free France in London. In this text, not reprinted in *Discours et Messages*, he specified:

I should like to state our position with regard to the Constitution and the laws of the French Republic. The Constitution and the laws of the French Republic have been, as you know, violated. Violated by the invader and violated by the invader's accomplices in Vichy, every day. We Free French recognize none of these violations.

We are obliged, since no expression of the national sovereignty exists in France at present, to improvise a *de facto* authority which we possess as provisional trustees of the national patrimony. We have already formally stated, and I repeat here, that we regard this authority as a kind of delegation of the national interest, an authority that we exercise provisionally and that we will restore to the national representation as soon as one can be freely constituted.

De Gaulle assumed this legitimacy, offering no other proof than the situation in effect. And perhaps what this Cartesian also felt at the absolute nadir of the disaster was satisfaction at the *tabula rasa*. Everything had been pulled down, but everything deserved to be. And De Gaulle would rebuild everything, starting from nothing. Thus the *Ordinance concerning the new organization of the public powers of Free France*, which he presented on September 24, 1941, established the future Constitution of France, for everything was already contained in this cornerstone:

In the name of the French People and of the French Empire We, General de Gaulle,

Leader of the Free French,

Considering our ordinances of October 27 and November 12, 1940, together with our constitutional declaration of November 16, 1940;

Considering that the situation resulting from the state of war continues to prevent any gathering and any free expression of the national representation;

Considering that the Constitution and the laws of the French Republic have been and are still violated throughout the metropolitan territory and the Empire, as much by the enemy's action as by the usurpation of the authorities collaborating with him;

Considering that many proofs establish the fact that the great majority of the French nation, far from accepting a regime imposed by violence and treason, regards the authority of Free France as the expression of its wishes and its will;

Considering that by reason of the growing importance of the territories of the French Empire and of the territories under French mandate, as well as of the French armed forces that have rallied to us to continue the war beside the Allies against the invader of the Nation, it is important that the authorities of Free France be in a position to exercise, *de facto* and provisionally, the normal attributions of the public powers;

We decree:

Article 1—By reason of the circumstances of the war and until there can be constituted a representation of the French people enabled to express the national will in a manner independent of the enemy, the provisional exercise of the public powers will be pursued in the conditions fixed by the present ordinance.

Article 2—There is established a National Committee composed of members appointed by decree. General de Gaulle, leader of the Free French, is president of the National Committee . . .

. . . In all, thirteen articles, one of which provides for the subsequent session of a Consultative Assembly. The "ordinances" cost De Gaulle less than Charles X. "Ordinance" is a word that did not intimidate him: between 1940 and 1946, he promulgated laws in this form in the name of the Provisional Government of the French Republic. If I have quoted at some length the beginning of the Ordinance of September 24, 1941, it is to recall that, at this period, the general gave an official and legal character to the organization of the *de facto* government which he represented. Hence the last article of the Ordinance called for its publication in the *Journal officiel de la France Libre*.

On October 2, 1941, during a luncheon given for him by the international press, De Gaulle said:

To organize and direct resistance, not only in the territories already liberated, but especially in France and in the Empire—this is the primary task the French National Committee has taken for its own. It will do so by delegation from the People who approve of it and to whom it will render an accounting. It will do so by uniting the nation in the war effort for liberation without excluding anyone except those who exclude themselves. It will do so in the conviction that the cause of France, I mean the restoration of her integrity, her independence, and her greatness, is at the same time the cause of all peoples fighting, as she is, for freedom. It will do so in the desire to fight without reservation side by side with her allies until the chronic evil of Germanism is crushed once and for all. It will do so in the hope that the solidarity of

nations will survive the ordeal and enable each man in the world
to live and die having experienced the sweetness of liberty.

This was not an oratorical effect: for De Gaulle, France's
freedom in the world is a touchstone, and everything else
follows from it. It still follows twenty years later, with partners who have privately decided that France is finished.
This has always been the difficulty with the Anglo-Americans, who are just beginning to understand. In London, at
the beginning of his speech in the Albert Hall on June 18,
1942, De Gaulle exclaimed:

We have chosen the hardest course, but also the best. Since
we have begun our task of national liberation and public salvation, not one of our actions, not one of our words has ever deviated from the line we have adopted. It is now June 18, 1942. I
myself am quite ready to repeat unchanged all we have done
and all we have said since June 18, 1940. I do not know if, elsewhere in the world, many attitudes and many declarations are
likely to be reconfirmed in their entirety by their authors after
two years. But I know that our own undertaking, from its first
hour, can be countersigned as it stands every single day.

Twenty-four years later, we can say that not one of his
actions, not one of his words has ever deviated from the line
that De Gaulle, once and for all, adopted. He has never acknowledged making a mistake on any point. In private life,
I prefer fallible beings who know themselves to be so. In
politics, the false great man apes Providence. The true great
man discerns in events and circumstances what must come
to pass and what will come to resemble him, for he will mark
it with his sign. In this, De Gaulle is inimitable.

He had already determined what he would propose to the
nation, and divined what the nation would decide when its
voice could be raised. To a journalist who asked him in London, during the May 27, 1942, press conference, if he intended "to convene Parliament, or to take other measures
with regard to the various political parties," he replied:

My personal opinion is that France will seek a new Assembly. Frankly, I do not believe (this is my personal opinion) that the old Parliament, which moreover abdicated when it voted in the Vichy Constitution, can be considered after the war as actually representing the French people. I believe that the French people will unanimously ask that a new Assembly, a national Convention, be held in order to express its will. I hope it will be constitutionally possible to find a means of linking the new French National Assembly to what existed formerly. . . . But as for the representation of the French people after this war, the general opinion of the French, and my own, is that the former Parliament will no longer represent them, for that former Parliament abdicated in the famous Vichy Assembly which granted Marshal Pétain the right to make a new Constitution.

We have seen how well De Gaulle knew the *general opinion of the French,* the reports he received from occupied or so-called "free" France—which was the opposite of Free France—that confirmed what he had known since June 1940 in the rebellion and refusal of his mind and heart. The opinion of the French that he accepted was the opinion that agreed with his own. The opinion of France, for De Gaulle, is always the opinion France will receive (is receiving) from him. France thinks, experiences, feels *through* Charles de Gaulle. On April 20, 1943, he made this clear:

Despite its terrible ordeals, our people know, and feel, that they are sufficiently rich in ideas, in experience and strength, to rebuild, as they mean to do, the structure of their future. This structure will be a new one. On every battlefield, in every kind of suffering, where their mission and their struggle are reforging a lucid and fraternal people, the immense majority of Frenchmen have decided that once the sun of freedom has reappeared, they will take a new road toward new horizons.

Certainly the nation, which knows no sovereign but itself, insists that, as its liberation advances, the laws it has formerly decreed be restored. Certainly the nation intends that every inch of its territory, once liberated, be swept clean of that caricature of fascism by which Vichy has disfigured it. But the nation has also condemned the political impotence, the social disequilibrium, and the moral bankruptcy that paralyzed the regime identified with its disaster. . . .

A true democracy, in which neither the maneuvers of professionals nor the morasses of intrigue disturb the functioning of national representation; in which, at the same time, the executive power, which has received its mandate from the people, possesses in itself the enduring strength to acquit itself of its duties in a manner worthy of France: that is the goal of the nation.

Enduring strength, that is the only problem. Three months before the long-awaited electoral consultation, De Gaulle, faithful to his promise, addressed the liberated and victorious nation in his broadcast speech of July 12, 1945:

It is the responsibility of the nation to say if the Third Republic's institutions have ceased to be valid. It was not the French people that destroyed them, but the invasion and its consequences. No one is qualified to pronounce them null and void except that people itself. In October, we shall all vote, in direct and universal suffrage, in order to elect an Assembly, and we shall say whether this Assembly is constituent—in other words, whether it has the mandate to work out a new Constitution.

If the majority of the voters decide negatively, it will mean that the former Constitution remains in force. The Assembly we have elected will then be the Chamber of Deputies. It will proceed at once to elect a Senate. After that, Chamber and Senate will reunite as the National Assembly to change the Constitution of 1875.

If, on the other hand, the voters decide by a majority that the Assembly is constituent, it will mean that they consider the Constitution in force before 1940 null and void.

De Gaulle believed that "there is an almost complete unanimity of good sense and feeling among our people about the principal changes that must be made in the future Constitution, in comparison to that of 1875." He was therefore content merely to raise the question, quite objectively. "When the time comes, and it will be soon, I shall give my own opinion on the subject." This opinion has not changed. It is the same opinion he made known in London on May 27, 1942.

Most members of the Consultative Assembly apparently identifying referendum with plebiscite (whereas De Gaulle declared that "what is proposed is precisely the contrary"), the general, in a declaration before the Assembly on July 29, 1945, after opposing the establishment of a sovereign Constituent Assembly which would risk "leading the democracy from abuse to abuse, to the brink of the abyss," concluded his appearance with these words:

I ask your indulgence to speak a few words of a personal nature, alas, before leaving the rostrum. I do this partly perhaps because many of the speeches we have heard here have, in effect prompted me to, but chiefly because I feel that it has become necessary, if we are ever to throw light on this debate. For myself —and I beg you to believe me—I cherish no ambition but the honor of leading France from the depths of the abyss to the moment when, victorious and free, she once again rules her own destiny. Yet how can I continue to the end of my task, if on so grave an issue, and one that is to me a matter of national conscience, I see the representatives of those who were my companions in that task take a position so divergent from my own? I do not say this to influence you in any decision you may make. For you, too, the question is one of conscience. I say this simply so that you will know all the elements of the problem that you will have to decide solely in the interests of the nation.

By a vote of 185 to 46, the Consultative Assembly rejected the government's plan and demanded a sovereign Constituent Assembly.

On October 17, 1945, four days before the referendum and the elections, De Gaulle announced in a broadcast what he regarded as the desirable choice:

Frenchmen, Frenchwomen, at this moment when you are about to go to the polls, I myself am ready, with all the members of the government, to hand over to the national representation, as I have always sworn I would, the exceptional powers I have exercised since June 18, 1940, in the name of the Republic, for the safeguarding of the State, and in the interests of France. Once more, I feel I must explain to every one of you my understanding of the national interest, the only interest I have ever served. . . .

With regard to the referendum, I hope with all my heart that you will answer "yes" to the first question and "yes" to the second. On the one hand, it is in my opinion absolutely essential that you express your desire for a new Republic, which we could not have if we returned to a regime that revealed its weakness during the country's great distress. But a new Republic does not exclude the possibility of a two-Assembly system. On the other hand, it is again my opinion that it is absolutely necessary, in order to obviate the arbitrary and the fortuitous, that the functioning of public authority—the Assembly and the Government—be in the main settled, while we await the Constitution, which must be worked out as quickly as possible and submitted to the approval of the people.

An overpowering majority dismissed the institutions of 1875; moreover, 66.3 per cent of the votes answered "yes" to the second question.

Elected President of the Provisional Government of the Republic by unanimous vote on November 13, 1945, De Gaulle, after asserting that "to a citizen such as himself, the vote of the Constituent National Assembly is an extreme honor," declared:

There is no question but that the executive power must account for its actions to the national representation; the latter must also accept its composition. At the same time, however, the government's independence, cohesion, and authority must be equal to the demands of its task. I would not feel I had the right to form or lead a government that was not sure of this authority, cohesion, and independence. It is a question of conscience. . . . Let us be explicit in this matter: we are about to make a decisive test of the representative system.

Not five days had passed before the general, who intended to form a government of national unanimity, threatened to withdraw. The Communists had, in effect, stipulated as a condition of their participation that one of the three key ministries (Foreign Affairs, War, Interior) be given to them. On November 17, De Gaulle explained his decision to the nation in a broadcast speech:

I have not been able to accept these conditions. . . . That is why, conforming to the principles of the representative system which we hope to see revived, and which has the right and duty to make decisions, I now turn again to the national representation and restore to it the mandate it entrusted to me.

The Assembly confirmed the President of the Provisional Government in his mandate. But everyone knew (or should have known) that he would remain in power only as long as he considered himself in a position to exercise it.

Twelve years later, on the night of June 2, 1958, but in an altogether different climate of opinion, and when he had only just returned to affairs of State, De Gaulle offered the deputies the same alternative in similar terms:

What is primary, ladies and gentlemen, in the decision that has led me to accept this task and, thanks to your investiture, to constitute this government; what has primarily guided me, as I may tell you in all frankness, is, in today's grave events (which confront us with the possibility of a general subversion of the nation) the determination to reform what must be reformed, starting with the present institutions—provided, of course, that the Parliament gives me and my government both the mandate and the means to do so.

You do not give this government the mandate and the means when you confront it with a complete change of the plan it has had the honor to submit to you.

Ladies and gentlemen—and I am weighing my words—the government cannot accept what is proposed to you by your Universal Suffrage Committee. . . .

The circumstances are such that the government cannot exercise its responsibilities beyond the present night, should matters be so decided. It will then take the necessary steps.

In conclusion, General de Gaulle thanked the deputies in advance with a remark that also recalled the words he addressed to the members of the National Constituent Assembly the day he had been unanimously elected President of the Provisional Government. What he said on November 13, 1945, he repeated on the night of June 2, 1958: "If you indicate your confidence in the government, the man who is speaking to you now will bear the honor of it for the rest of his life." The vote this time was 350 to 161.

More recently, De Gaulle has taxed not the deputies, but the nation itself with its responsibilities. Once again he let it be understood that he would leave office if he was not supported. This was in October 1962, when he proposed to the nation that henceforth the President of the Republic be elected by universal suffrage. On October 4, he concluded his televised address: "It is your answers that, on October 28, will tell me if I can and if I must continue my labors in the service of France." And, more categorically, on October 18:

If your answer is "No!", which is the choice of all the old parties in order to re-establish their disastrous regime, the choice of all the factions eager to fling themselves into subversion; or even if the majority of affirmative votes is slight and therefore hazardous, it is quite obvious that my task will be ended at once and irremediably. For what could I do, subsequently, without the warm confidence of the nation?

Finally, on October 26:

Now our Constitution, in order to function effectively, requires that the chief of State be precisely that. For four years, I have held this position. It is up to the French people to say, next Sunday, whether I am to continue. . . . I am sure that you will say "Yes," because you feel that if the French nation, in its own eyes and in the eyes of the world, were to deny De Gaulle, or were even to accord him merely a vague and dubious confidence, his historical task would immediately be impossible and, consequently, concluded; but that on the contrary he may and must pursue that task if, en masse, you desire it.

This was the moment toward which De Gaulle had been heading for years. This had been his deepest thought, his profoundest desire: France would be saved, on the day she had a leader, on the day she was no longer the *headless woman*. Though what he was, what he is, what he has never ceased being, remains the guarantee of what De Gaulle will be; though what he has always said and done should make it possible to be prepared for what he will say and do; nonetheless, De Gaulle often amazes those whose profession and interest it is to attempt to foresee the political future, both remote and immediate. What the nation would understand on October 28, 1962, its representatives and the nation itself did not realize on December 31, 1945, when De Gaulle had already been just as explicit.

To our political fauna, he appears as a creature of another species: they sniff at him with anxiety and hostility, but are disarmed. De Gaulle is immune to parties. First of all because he has long been unintelligible to them. They do not understand him. When he withdrew, on January 20, 1946, the surprise was enormous. But our surprise at the time is what now seems surprising to us. A few days earlier, on December 31, 1945, during the discussion of the National Defense budget and the forty-hour debate to which it gave rise, the general made two declarations before the National Constituent Assembly, in which he announced his intentions in a manner that could not be clearer. I have already quoted the first. At the end of the second, he specified:

Do we want a government that will really govern, or is it preferable to have an all-powerful Assembly that merely uses the government to carry out its wishes? The second solution has sometimes been tried by us, and it has also been tried by others.

I am personally convinced that it does not correspond in any way to the needs of the country in which we live and to the times in which we live. The problems we face are so numerous, so complex, so precipitate and so cruel that it would be impossible to solve them in such a constitutional framework.

Then what form should the government take? I do not speak for myself, naturally, but for you—but I hasten to speak while I still can.

The best formula for a government, in my opinion, after all the experiments we have made, is that of a body that alone holds and wields—I repeat, alone wields—the entire responsibility of executive power.

If the Assembly, or the Assemblies, refuse the government all or part of the powers it judges necessary for executive responsibility, it resigns and another government takes over. And that is exactly what is about to happen, it seems to me . . .

". . . And doubtless this is the last time I shall be speaking to you from this place . . ."; ". . . I hasten to speak while I still can . . ."; ". . . another government takes over. And that is exactly what is about to happen, it seems to me . . ." He could not be clearer. And yet when he withdrew, twenty days later, his resignation seemed incomprehensible, even scandalous. De Gaulle comments, in his *War Memoirs:*

The order of the day, adopted virtually unanimously by the Assembly, imposed no conditions upon me. After which, the budget was passed without difficulty. But although my defeat had not been effected, the mere fact that it had appeared possible produced a profound effect. My government had been breached by the majority during a threat-crammed debate. Henceforth, perhaps, the same thing could be accomplished apropos of virtually any issue. It was apparent that if De Gaulle tolerated this situation in order to remain in office, his prestige would decline, until one day the parties would either no longer tolerate him or else relegate him to some harmless and decorative function. But I had neither the right nor the inclination to lend myself to such calculations. As I left the Palais Bourbon on the evening of January 1, I had determined upon my departure from office. All that remained was to select the date, without making any concessions whatever.

Certainly it would be before the end of the month. For the constitutional debate would then begin, and I was convinced that by remaining in the nascent regime, I would not have the possibility of imposing my views nor even of supporting them (III, p. 319).

No other remedy but the removal of De Gaulle by De Gaulle: this would be a comic performance on anyone else's part, but not on De Gaulle's. It is as if he were saying: I am leaving, and you will recall me in order not to perish, though you detest me and although I threaten you unduly . . .

He withdrew. He kept silence. Not for long. On May 12, 1946, during the celebration of both the national holiday of Joan of Arc and the first anniversary of victory, he went to pay his respects to the grave of Georges Clemenceau—to whom he had addressed himself from London, on November 11, 1941: "When the victory is won, when justice has been done, the French will come and tell you so. Then, with all the dead that lie in the earth of France, you can sleep in peace." The French? At least the man who represents them: he will suffice, though he has left power. Hence he went to the Vendée grave, and he said:

The example of Clemenceau, unshakable amid the storm, intransigent in his faith in France, tirelessly devoted to the cause of liberty, growing only the more ardent as he saw more souls yield, more hearts soften—how greatly he influenced the decisions of those who in the course of this war were responsible for leading the State out of the depths of the abyss!

President Clemenceau! When the enemy crushed your country, we swore to be loyal to your example. History will say if the promise was kept. But we also promised to come, once victory was gained, to thank you for the lessons you taught us.

De Gaulle spoke of Clemenceau—which was a discreet way of speaking of himself. And he spoke, already, of the French people as united, as *rassemblé;* for from a united people will come the State's salvation:

On the morrow of the recent ordeal, in which the nation's honor, unity, and very soul narrowly escaped perishing, we can measure, better than ever, the cost of our eternal inner demons which divide and mislead us.

At the moment when, ravaged yet victorious, we return to our path in a war-torn world, we see more clearly than ever that, tomorrow as yesterday, there can be no security, no freedom, no effectiveness without accepting great disciplines under the leadership of a strong State, in the ardor of a united people.

The word *rassemblement* was one that had long been familiar to De Gaulle, for it expressed his most constant preoccupation. In his commemorative speech of June 18, 1944, before the Consultative Assembly in Algiers, he spoke in this way of the effort and success of Free France, which had now become Fighting France:

But the national *rassemblement* for war, for freedom and for greatness, which the French began on June 18, 1940, and which subsequently, step by step, they pursued to its conclusion, involved, as the French knew well, enormous difficulties for their nation. An old people accustomed to the vicissitudes of history, they knew how arduous it is to scale the slope of the abyss. As a nation tested by long human experience, they knew that their best friends, however numerous throughout the world, would not always afford them immediate and unconditional support.

Let us note that the term, which predates the RPF, will survive it. It was in 1960 that De Gaulle declared, in Gap: "If we unite around France [*nous nous rassemblons sur la France*], so that she is truly France, our destiny is assured." And in Paris on August 25, 1964, he evoked those "elementary guarantees—a solid State, a modern defense, and a united [*rassemblée*] nation.

This is a necessary illusion. What is there in common between one Frenchman and another? Between De Gaulle and Sartre? Between Breton and Maritain? Not one taste, not one tendency, not one idea. Sartre, as soon as he speaks of De Gaulle, is no longer Sartre. One does not *rassembler* the

French, except in speeches; but also sometimes—and this is the essential thing—in ballots. Hail, Number, you are the god who loves De Gaulle and who preserves him for us!

On June 14, 1944, De Gaulle, visiting the bridgehead of the Normandy landing, had been welcomed by the authorities in Bayeux, where he was "eager to indicate without delay that wherever the enemy had retreated, the authority now proceeded from my government." He describes the situation thus in his *Memoirs:*

We proceeded on foot, from street to street. At the sight of General de Gaulle, the inhabitants stood in a kind of daze, then burst into bravos or else into tears. Rushing out of their houses, they followed after me, all in the grip of an extraordinary emotion. The children surrounded me. The women smiled and sobbed. The men shook my hand. We walked on together, all overwhelmed by comradeship, feeling national joy, pride and hope rise again from the depths of the abyss. . . . All those who held any office, wielded any power, or fulfilled any function rushed up to greet me (II, p. 260).

Two years later, De Gaulle, who had already withdrawn from the government, returned to Bayeux to preside over the festivities commemorating his visit of June 1944. On that June 16, 1946, he declared:

It is here on the soil of our ancestors that the State was reborn! A legitimate State, since it was founded on the interests and the feelings of the nation; a State whose true sovereignty had been restored to the party of combat, of liberty, and of victory, while servitude maintained only the appearance of sovereignty; a State upheld in its rights, its dignity, and its authority amid the vicissitudes of destitution and intrigue; a State saved from the interference of foreign powers; a State that was able to re-establish around itself both national unity and imperial unity, to muster all the forces of the country and of the French Union, to carry the victory to its conclusion at the side of its allies, to negotiate as an equal with the other great nations of the world, to maintain public order, to mete out justice, and to begin our reconstruction.

He sketched the major outlines of the re-established but still to be renovated State in this speeech in Bayeux; "all our principles and all our experience show that the legislative, executive, and judicial powers should be clearly divided and soundly balanced, and that above political contingencies there should be a national arbiter to establish continuity among the coalitions":

It is therefore from the head of the State, placed above party feeling, elected by a college that includes the Parliament, but with a wider scope and composed in such a way as to make him President of the French Union as well as of the French Republic —it is from him that the executive power must proceed. It must be his task to reconcile the general interest as to the choice of men with the orientation of the Parliament itself. It must be his task to appoint the ministers and first of all, of course, the Prime Minister [le Premier] who is to direct the policy and work of the government. It must be his task to promulgate laws and decrees, for these commit the citizens toward the State as a whole. It must be his task to preside over the Councils of the government, and to ensure that continuity a nation cannot do without. It must be his task to act as arbiter in any political contingency, either normally through the Council, or in moments of grave confusion by calling on the country to make its sovereign wishes known by means of elections. It must be his task, if the nation is in danger, to safeguard national independence and the treaties concluded by France.

In its broad outlines, the Constitution De Gaulle had desired since the forties would be this very one which, after many vicissitudes and a long wait, he would finally cause to be adopted. Of course, if we find him anticipating a Prime Minister in Bayeux, many details cannot yet be foreseen and must be changed. The De Gaulle who on June 16, 1946, spoke as follows was aware of the fact:

The future of the 110 million men and women who live in the shadow of our flag is in a federal organization, which time will gradually evolve, but the new Constitution must initiate it and organize its development.

The invitation to the *rassemblement,* first trace of a decision he perhaps hoped was not yet inevitable, and which he announced in Strasbourg on April 7 of the following year, can be found again, even earlier, at the end of the Bayeux speech:

Let us be lucid and strong enough both to create and to observe the rules of national life that will tend to unite us [*nous rassembler*] at a time when we are ceaselessly driven to division among ourselves! Our whole history is the alternation of the immense sorrows of a divided people and the fruitful greatness of a free nation mustered under the aegis of a strong State.

A free nation—only today are we beginning to understand what De Gaulle meant by that; we have known for six years what he meant by a strong State. Yet this is a simplistic view, in that it does not take into account the social conflict; as if a nation existed only politically. There is another history. But De Gaulle would deny this. For the other history to be possible, a people's conditions of existence must first be assured; today, these conditions are political, and they are as De Gaulle has defined them.

Questions of terminology are important—for they imply with precision the extent of the government's powers. Commenting in his declaration of August 27, 1946, on the draft of a Constitution being considered by the National Constituent Assembly, De Gaulle said:

We must note first of all that the text of the draft does not even contain the words "government" or "executive power." Mention is made only of the "council of ministers" or of the "cabinet." Yet it is the notion of governing, with all it implies of the capacity to act, and not only to deliberate, that it is essential to emphasize in the very terms of the document.

After reminding his hearers in this same text: "Our previous political system collapsed in an ordeal which it was able neither to foresee, prevent, nor control. Nothing is more necessary for our country than to organize the State in such a fashion that it will possess, in its structure, sufficient strength; in its functioning, sufficient effectiveness; in its personnel, sufficient prestige to lead the nation and assure its salvation, whatever may happen," De Gaulle added:

In truth, it is from the President of the Republic that the government must proceed in all circumstances. . . .

There is something strange about the fact that the draft grants the head of the State only functions that, in practice, are quite inoperative, while theoretically making him a representative of the permanent interests of the French Union and an arbiter placed above parties. . . .

By denying the head of the State the means of assuring the regular functioning of institutions, of governing the nation effectively, of emphasizing the permanent interests of France, of serving as a living link between metropolitan France and the overseas territories, of being, as a result the safeguard, whatever may happen, of national independence, territorial integrity, and the treaties signed by France, we risk forcing the State into a confusion of powers and responsibilities even worse than that which led the previous regime to disaster and to abdication.

On the night of September 28, 1946, the Assembly approved the draft of the Constitution, which the nation would accept or reject by referendum. On October 13, De Gaulle spoke at Épinal. There he first reminded his audience that "the very day we undertook our mission in the service of France, we made and proclaimed this pledge . . . that once the liberation of the country was achieved and victory won, we would restore complete self-determination to the French people":

In this there was on our part, first of all, a conviction as firm as it was reasoned. Further, in a conflict that represented, for

France, the ideological struggle between totalitarianism and freedom, to betray her ideal would have been to deny, that is, to destroy her very self. Finally, in doing battle for the rights of the nation, internal rights as well as external ones, we gave our action and our authority the character of legitimacy; we were safeguarding for all Frenchmen the terrain on which they could recover their national unity, and we put ourselves in a position to meet all attempts at alien encroachment with a justified intransigence. The pledge we made we have, purely and simply, kept.

In short, "the Republic has been saved at the same time as the nation. . . . But if the Republic is saved, it remains to rebuild it." And De Gaulle, once again, explained what he believed the Constitution must be. He was aware of reiterating what he had already said: "We repeat today what we have not ceased saying in many forms and on many occasions": the separation of powers; the establishment "of a head of State who is really that," of a Parliament that is genuine, of a "justice that will be justice," of a "French Union that will be a union and that will be French":

For ourselves, we declare that, despite some progress over the preceding one, the draft of the Constitution approved last night by the National Assembly is not satisfactory. Moreover, it would surprise us if it should seem so to many of those who voted for it for reasons quite remote, no doubt, from the constitutional problem itself. For it is one of the strange characteristics of political life today that questions are dealt with not directly, and as they really exist, but from the angle of what is conventionally called "tactics," a policy that occasionally leads, it appears, to abandoning the positions one has sworn to defend. But we, who do not practice so obscure an art, and who believe, on the contrary, that for France nothing is more important than to restore as swiftly as possible the effectiveness and the authority of the republican State—we believe that the present result cannot be approved because it does not correspond to the necessary conditions. . . .

For after all, when it is clear to everyone how greatly the State is hampered by both the omnipotence and the division of the parties, is it wise to permit these same parties to possess, *de facto* and directly, at their own discretion and without counterbalance, all the powers of the Republic? . . .

But on October 13, the Constitution was approved by a vote of 9,263,416 to 8,143,981; there were 8,467,537 abstentions.

Foreshadowed at Bruneval on March 30, 1947 ("The day will come when, casting aside the sterile maneuvers of party policy and forming anew the unwieldy structure of leadership in which the nation has lost its purpose and the State been disqualified, the enormous majority of the French will unite [se rassemblera] around France"), the Rassemblement du Peuple Français is launched in Strasbourg the following April 7:

We all know what has happened. The Constitution, according to which all powers are to derive from, and in their functioning depend directly and exclusively on, the parties and their coalitions, has been accepted by nine million electors, rejected by eight million, and ignored by eight million. But it has been adopted! We may note today what its results have been. Let us avoid blaming the men involved, some of whom are—and I say so from my own experience—highly worthy and highly capable of leading the various branches of public affairs, but who have been misled or paralyzed by the system itself. In any case, it is clear that the nation does not have to guide a State whose cohesion, effectiveness, and authority enable it to deal with the problems that face it. . . .

Now we must boldly face our dilemma, and by a long and persevering effort, solve the problems that threaten our life and our greatness as a nation. The cause is now clear, and we shall not prevail by dividing ourselves into rigid and opposing categories. . . .

It is time that those Frenchmen and Frenchwomen who think and feel this way—that is, I am convinced, the enormous majority of our people—unite to prove it. It is time that we form and organize the Rassemblement du Peuple Français which, in the context of law and order, will promote and bring to victory, beyond all differences of opinion, the great effort of common salvation and the profound reform of the State. Thus, tomorrow, in a new accord of action and resolve, the French Republic will construct the new France!

One of the most surprising things about De Gaulle is certainly his faculty for "starting over." He begins from scratch again as often as he must. That he has achieved his goal in regard to the Constitution seems indeed incredible when we consider habits of mind, interests at stake, parliamentary prejudices. De Gaulle imposes upon the French political milieu all that it detests and fears most. This is a unique tour de force in our history. The Left has supposed that the Right would get rid of him by assassination. But ever since our Ravaillacs have graduated from the École Polytechnique, they have missed their targets. And De Gaulle has a clear field to do what he has to do.

In his first declaration of December 31, 1945, against the Assembly regime, the general predicted "a situation that will make you bitterly regret the course you have chosen to take." Once again, De Gaulle prophesied accurately. He had foreseen everything, except the length of the interim. It took twelve years, not for this prediction to appear well-founded, but for it to be fulfilled. Twelve years during which the State lost more and more of its substance and which ended on May 13, 1958. It was in order to accelerate a development too slow for his taste that the general was led to intervene, first on June 16, 1946, in his speech at Bayeux, then by increasingly frequent discussions of his position, and finally by the creation of the RPF. De Gaulle, imperturbable, convinced he was right, did not anticipate that France could do without him more than a few days. But his mistake proved the truth of his doctrine: we were sliding down the slope once again, and once again beginning to die day after day; and we were stopped at the penultimate second by De Gaulle, who caught us on the brink of the void.

During his press conference at the Maison de la Résistance alliée, on April 24, 1947, a few days after the creation of the RPF, De Gaulle declared:

Given the parties as they exist in France today, I regard it as indispensable that the powers be separated according to a basic democratic principle. The legislative power is one thing. The executive power is another. This does not mean, of course, that the government is not accountable for its actions to the national representation. But the two powers must have a common and direct source, which is the French people. Otherwise we would remain in the situation that constrains us now, in which the legislative and executive powers are at the discretion of the parties, and we can neither define nor pursue a policy. The separation of powers is at the basis of any democracy. But I believe that for France, given our divisions, which are, unfortunately, deep and many, the separation of powers is an absolute necessity if we wish to prevent the parties from splitting not only the government but all the workings of the State; if we wish to prevent, ultimately, a situation in which no one serves the State but in which everyone serves a party.

On October 5, 1947, in Vincennes, he exclaimed:

Frenchmen, Frenchwomen, it is your responsibility to unite, as I ask, to reform the State by wresting it from the sterile discretion of the parties and enabling it to guide the nation with no consideration except the common interest; to support with discipline the action of recovery, which renewed public powers can and must undertake; to repulse, while there is still time, this kind of invasion-before-the-fact effected by the separatists.

The separatists were the communists. We must not forget the danger the Soviet Union represented at the time. The following October 27, after municipal elections which "doomed the regime of confusion and division that plunges the State into impotence," De Gaulle, demanding the dissolution of the National Assembly and new elections, announced: "Events are too threatening for any delay to be permissible. Everyone knows that the State, as it is constituted and as it is led, risks collapsing in ruin and anarchy, the habitual prelude of invasions." These words, at this date, had a meaning clear to everyone.

The general's error was to hope that by creating the RPF he was doing more than adding one more party to the rest. He assumed he could "unite" [*rassembler*] Frenchmen of all opinions, Right or Left, as in the days of the Resistance.

One of the propaganda themes De Gaulle exploited at this time and on which he relied to bring him to power, was the capital-labor Association. He had often spoken, in the heroic days of Free France, of the renovation, even the revolution that the Liberation would effect. In one of his first broadcast speeches from London, on August 3, 1940, he evoked "this great war which is also a great revolution," and specified, at the same microphone, on the following November 29:

From this certain victory, from our victory, we Free French seek to create a new France. Such a war is a revolution, the greatest the world has ever known. What we, we Free French contribute, what we provide that is active, great, and pure, we would make into a leaven. We Free French seek to reap, one day, a tremendous harvest of devotion, of disinterestedness, of mutual aid. That is how, tomorrow, France will live again.

And on November 15, 1941, in his Albert Hall speech:

If it is possible to say that this war is a revolution, this is more true for France than for any other nation. A nation that pays so dearly for the faults of its political, social, and moral regime and for the failure or felony of so many leaders; a nation that suffers so cruelly the effects of the physical and moral disintegration worked within it by the enemy and his collaborators; a nation whose men, women, and children are hungry, poorly dressed, without heat, two million of whose young men have been held captive for months and years in barracks, concentration camps, prisons, or cells; a nation that has been offered, as solution and as hope, only forced labor in the enemy's service, combat against her own sons and her loyal allies, the regret of having dared to oppose Hitler's conquering frenzies, and ritual prostrations before the image of Father Defeat—this nation is perforce a bed of glowing coals under the ashes. There is not the slightest doubt that, after the terrible crisis it is traversing, the French nation will experience a vast renewal.

In London, on April 1, 1942, at the dinner of the "National Defense Public Interest Committee," alluding to the "absurd snobbery" of his allies' concern over not seeing on the rosters of Fighting France "many names formerly so respected," De Gaulle exclaimed that "this is first of all a cruel injustice to so many illustrious men who, in France and outside France, live only for victory," and added:

But it is, above all, the serious neglect of a fact that today dominates the entire French question—a fact called "revolution". For it is a revolution, the greatest of her history, that France, betrayed by her elite groups and her privileged classes, has begun to institute. And I must say, in this regard, that the people throughout the world who imagine that they may again find, after the last shot is fired, a France politically, socially, morally similar to the France they once knew, will be committing a signal error. In the secrecy of her grief, at this very moment, an entirely new France is being created, whose guides will be new men. Those who are surprised at not finding among us stereotyped politicians, somnolent academicians, scheming businessmen, status-drained generals, remind us of those backward followers in the petty courts of Europe who, during the last French Revolution, were offended at not seeing Turgot, Necker, and Loménie de Brienne sitting on the Committee of Public Safety. What can you expect! A revolutionary France still prefers to win the war with General Hoche rather than to lose it with Marshal de Soubise. In order to proclaim and impose the Declaration of Rights, a revolutionary France still prefers to listen to Danton rather than to doze through the droning formulas of the past.

This sounds splendid in De Gaulle's mouth, but is it true? Where are the revolutionaries, aside from himself? All the others, no matter which party of the Right or Left they belong to, have but one desire: to change nothing. De Gaulle alone demands the reform of institutions, against all the parties in league against him. And they all, in his eyes, stand for what must be dominated, if not destroyed.

In any case, on May 27, 1942, De Gaulle did not hesitate, in the press conference already cited, to call the Assembly that was to convene after the Liberation a National Convention. On Radio London, on April 20, 1943, he heralded:

An economic and social regime in which no monopoly and no coalition can influence the State or decide the fate of individuals; in which, consequently, the chief sources of common wealth are either administered or at least controlled by the nation; in which each Frenchman has the opportunity to work according to his aptitudes under conditions capable of insuring a decent existence to himself and his family; in which free groups of laborers and technicians are organically associated with the progress of business—such is the fruitful reform with which the renewed nation seeks to console its children.

On the following May first, in his brief Labor Day message:

When victory comes, the grateful nation must and will be able to offer its children—workers, artisans, farmers—first of all a decent and secure lot in life, and subsequently the place that is their due in the management of the great common interests.

In Algiers, on November 3, 1943, during the inaugural session of the provisional Consultative Assembly:

France has suffered too many ordeals and learned too much about both herself and others not to have resolved to effect profound transformations. She will insist that national sovereignty be exercised integrally, without the distortions of intrigue and without the corrupting pressures of any coalition of private interests. She will insist that the men she appoints to govern have the means to do so with sufficient power and continuity to impose the supreme power of the State on all within the nation, and to pursue intentions worthy of herself outside the nation. She will insist on the end of an economic regime in which the great sources of national production and distribution have been outside her control, where corporate management has excluded the participation of the labor organizations on which she, however, depended.

"Doubtless the nation will determine these great reforms itself," he added then. We know the time it has taken, even to reach the political objective.

In Algiers again, on March 18, 1944, before the provisional Consultative Assembly, De Gaulle specified:

It is a democracy renewed in its structure and especially in its practice that our people demands. . . . But French democracy must be a social democracy, that is, ensuring each man the organic right and liberty to work, guaranteeing the dignity and security of all in an economic system designed to develop national resources, and not to benefit private interests; a democracy in which the great sources of the common wealth will belong to the nation, in which the direction and control of the State will be exercised with the regular co-operation of labor and capital. Lastly, the highest intellectual and moral values, on which the deepest resources and influence of the nation depend, must be able to collaborate directly with the government.

From Algiers, on that March 18, 1944, De Gaulle had forewarned his countrymen: "It is, of course, painful to tell the nation, which has suffered so severely, that the arrival of the French and Allied forces will not mark the beginning of euphoria." Therefore he spoke chiefly of the effort that remained to be made in his speech of September 12, 1944, which profoundly disappointed the fervent crowd of Resistance fighters that constituted his audience. Nevertheless he said:

We can see clearly enough to determine to take a new course what the negligence, mediocrity, injustice that we have practiced or tolerated, and also, let us admit, the lack of boldness and continuity in initiative and direction in public office have, before and during this drama, cost our power, our unity, our very substance.

To summarize the principles that France henceforth means to make the basis of her national activity, we will say that, while assuring the maximum possible freedom and favoring the spirit of enterprise in every matter, France expects private interest to yield to the common good; the great sources of common wealth to be developed and directed not to the profit of a few, but to the advantage of all; the coalitions of interests, which have so burdened the condition of men and the policy of the State itself, to be abolished once and for all; and, finally, each of her sons and daughters to be able to live, work, and raise their children in security and dignity.

Let us admit . . . He had already admitted it often; he was to admit it often again, as long as necessary until something could be done about it. The issue was whether De Gaulle's will and thought were to become the will and thought of France. If the revolution in question were to be chiefly political—and the general insisted that it be effected within a context of law and order—he was also determined that it be, to some degree, social. In Lille, on October 1, 1944, he advocated "the collaboration between labor and management." Discreetly, De Gaulle put the accent on collaboration with the workers, declaring in his broadcast of December 31, 1944:

Today, we must get used to and make the best of what we have, must endure restrictions and shortages with fortitude. But at the same time it is the duty of all of us participating in the sacred task of French production—heads of large concerns, engineers, workers, farmers—to create the methods and the atmosphere of a true and open collaboration through all the effort, initiative, temporary setback, and final success, which must comprise the new psychology of our national action. We must at the same time proceed with a certain number of basic reforms which correspond both to the needs of modern economy and to social progress.

We know what the post-Liberation governments did (and failed to do), beginning with that of the general who, applying the program of the CNR (Conseil National de la Résistance), nationalized credit, the major banks, the coal fields of the north and the Pas-de-Calais; prepared for the nationalization of those in the central region, the Midi, and Lorraine and for the nationalization of gas and electricity (voted shortly after De Gaulle's withdrawal); decided on the reorganization of Social Security; created Chambers of Commerce; and established a General Planning Commission.

In social policy, the RPF looked back to the promises of 1940–44. De Gaulle specified and developed these, insisted on collaboration between capital and labor, several hints of which we have already seen in the general's speeches from the days of London and Algiers. In Strasbourg, on April 7, 1947, De Gaulle declared:

Social action? Are we then condemned to that state of ruinous and exasperating uneasiness in which the men working together within the same enterprise find their interests and their sentiments in conflict? Are we condemned forever to oscillate painfully between one system in which the workers are simple instruments in the enterprise of which they are a part, and another that would crush all men, body and soul, in an odious totalitarian and bureaucratic machinery? No! The human, French, and practical solution of this overriding question is neither in the abasement of some, nor in the servitude of all. It is in the worthy and fruitful association between those who invest, within a single enterprise, either their labor, their technology, or their wealth, and who should participate openly, as honest shareholders, in its profits and its risks.

This theme, the inspiration of the RPF, was developed in Lille on June 29, 1947; in Saint-Étienne on January 4; in

Marseilles, at the first National Sessions of the Rassemblement on April 17; in Paris, at the Vélodrome d'Hiver, on December 14, 1948; in Lille again, on February 12, 1949; in Paris, at the Bois de Boulogne parade grounds, on November 14; then on May 1, 1950. Finally, on June 25, 1950, during his speech closing the National Sessions of the Rassemblement du Peuple Français, he said:

The social lesion is gravest of all. . . . In this matter, we have made up our minds on the course to be followed. It is that of Association! Further, in its behalf we have begun to inspire among the masses a mystique of great power, the only mystique that can oppose the lure of the totalitarian abyss. I declare that we are ready to accomplish the great reform that will completely transform social relations and tremendously improve French productivity. It follows that we intend to apply Association to the enterprises that have been nationalized and, in large measure, to the public services. . . . But it is a genuine and contractual Association we seek to establish, and not such substitutes as premiums for productivity, workers' shareholding, and interest in profits, by which some, who consider themselves astute, attempt to evade it. In this matter, as in the others, there is no discrepancy between our actions and our intentions.

Time was short; the victory of the RPF was still not achieved, was becoming less and less likely. At the Vélodrome d'Hiver, on February 11, 1950, De Gaulle adjured those who refused to join the Rassemblement (of the million adherents it numbered in 1948, the RPF now possessed no more than three hundred and fifty thousand):

Join us! You who keep the national tradition alive, you who piously respect the foundations of the country, you who believe that France needs the accumulated treasure of her ancestors.

Join us! You who are still inspired by Christian faith, which sheds the light of love and brotherhood over the vale of human woes, which lights, from age to age, the spiritual torch of the nation . . .

Social justice, national tradition, Christian faith, the three beacons that alternately illuminate the history of France—they must burn now to show us the dark path, while our people, united for its salvation, marches unhesitatingly towards its destiny.

This was one of the rare moments when the politician spoke as a Christian, when Dante appeared behind Machiavelli. This was because in 1950 the danger was urgent: there was just enough time. Once again, our escape was a narrow one. The RPF, which I condemned (justifiably), was profoundly necessary. And in truth, it failed only in appearance. In the long run, it triumphed. Not only is it in power today, it has fundamentally changed our institutions, as De Gaulle wished. And this alone, ultimately, mattered to him: what would continue after him and make Gaullism a lasting phenomenon.

In his distress at seeing France lose her vital forces and waste the national capital that he himself represented, De Gaulle, in the RPF days, did not always avoid demagoguery, which is scarcely surprising. But if he promised the people more than he could give if he was returned to power, it was because he knew that, thanks to the renovation of the State, he would in the essentials assure it the indispensable conditions of its honor and happiness. At the Porte de Versailles, on June 25, 1950, he repeated what he has always said, what he will always say:

It is one of the most telling evidences of mediocrity in our time that men who, throughout the ordeal, swore to renew, first, the institutions and thereby the policy of our nation allowed themselves to be snared so rapidly in the maneuvers of the politicians. As a result, the parties restored their regime, deceiving the nation as to their intentions, aided by the press, business, and the trade-union associations—which accept only a State their coalitions can permeate—joined for the occasion with the separatists who permit the government strength only on condition that it belongs to them, and supported, finally, by the action and the

propaganda of the major foreign powers who were eager to revive
a malleable and divided France.

But as it was only too easy to foresee, the regime they resuscitated was openly inadequate to the problems that face the
world. Hence the more than a dozen parties no longer have any
influence over the masses, and in consequence are no more than
clans and sects. Doubtless they can, for a time, by sheer force of
habit, still retain local "electoral" positions. But the mainspring
is broken. No one supposes that any of them can henceforth
carry the people as a whole. They themselves do not believe it,
who in their pathetic congresses, noting the holes in their ranks
and the doubts of their partisans, think of nothing but thinking
again of themselves. As for the government, formed by the
juxtaposition of rivalries without arbitration, it is, of course,
sterile. Who can describe the lusterless apathy in which the councils of the successive governments and the sessions of Parliament
are conducted? To be sure, despite such official unsubstantiality,
the nation in the depths of its being is recovering some of its
substance, for a vigorous sap flows in this vital people. But it is
being led nowhere, and to nothing. No one supposes that in the
first difficulty to arise, the present regime could be the guide and
the recourse of France.

In this new venture, which was to end in failure, De
Gaulle counted the years, as was his custom—for example,
he declared on June 25, 1950, at the National Sessions of
the Rassemblement du Peuple Français: "It is three years
now since we have undertaken the second phase of our national task." The third phase, eight years later, would be the
successful one. But meanwhile, how many futile efforts and
disappointed hopes! Not quite futile, if it was true, as De
Gaulle often asserted at this period, that his presence at the
head of the RPF imposed a certain discretion upon the successive governments. This was what the general called, not
without irony, "the system of indirect government," the only
kind he could then lay claim to, remarking in the same
speech of June 25:

Nonetheless, despite the chloroform by which those in power seek to benumb it, the nation is distressed and disturbed by the void that yawns where the State should appear. That is why the parties continue to be obsessed by the hearing we ourselves receive from the people. The result is that the role we play at present offers some analogy with that of the Commander whose effigy troubled those whose conscience was not without reproach. The fear the parties have of us suffices to inspire in them certain impulses toward prudence. Whence their present tendency to violate their various programs and to belie their promises, in the hope of circumventing crises. It follows that the system is thereby merely immobilized further. But at least its paralysis avoids shocks; although not always, I am told!

Furthermore, as our appeals arouse the country, the parties, while still opposing us, are attempting to claim our objectives. The method is always the same. As soon as we show the nation a goal to achieve and the course by which to do so, first sniping and distorting criticisms are lavished upon it in the Assembly, the press, and on the radio. Then, gradually, once the project is suitably debaptized, it is claimed as their own. Suddenly, with a great burst of publicity-seeking self-congratulation, there is the pretense of seeking to implement it. If by chance, this is achieved, we should be the first to congratulate ourselves on the results achieved by the system of indirect government. Unfortunately, the copies made thus far are merely caricatures.

It was not General de Gaulle's fault if this development ended in a revolution less peaceful than he had hoped. The accession of the Fifth Republic was ineluctable, but it might have succeeded the Fourth without a break. The RPF, which was greeted so contemptuously at the time, appears entirely justified today. Once again the general was accused of dictatorial intentions, whereas he created the RPF merely in order to take power legally, to change the Constitution, and to govern democratically by means of a lasting majority. How much better it would have been if De Gaulle had triumphed by an electoral success of the Rassemblement, rather than as a result of the events in Algiers! On May 6,

1953, the general acknowledged the failure of the RPF in a declaration to the press:

Thus the effort that I have been leading since the war, surrounded by Frenchmen resolved that our country would find its unity at last and establish at its head a State that would truly be one, has not met with success. I acknowledge as much without equivocation. This is, I fear, to the detriment of France. . . . The occasion for a regrouping may come from a future popular consultation under very different conditions and in a profoundly altered atmosphere. It may come, too, from an impulse of popular opinion which, under the sway of anxiety, would lead the French to unite, and the regime to be transformed. But it risks, alas! appearing in the form of a serious shock, in which, once again, the supreme law would be the salvation of the nation and of the State. That would be the collapse of illusions. We must prepare the remedy.

He would intervene again only to oppose the project for the European Defense Community, and then return to silence.

FIVE YEARS later, the anticipated upheaval occurred, and the party regime, as foreseen, collapsed. On May 15, 1958, General de Gaulle published the following declaration:

The degradation of the State inevitably entails the withdrawal of associated peoples, unrest in the army, national dislocation, the loss of independence. For twelve years, France, at grips with problems too harsh for the party regime to solve, has been committed to this disastrous course.

In the past, the nation has made me feel that in the depths of its soul it trusted me to lead it to salvation.

Today, facing the ordeals that once again lie before it, the country knows that I am prepared to assume the powers of the Republic.

As Paul-Marie de la Gorce has remarked in his *De Gaulle entre deux Mondes*, "with time, it is easier to discern what, in this communiqué, heralded the future or revealed a state of mind. The word *Algérie* was not spoken; it was alluded to only by the phrase *associated peoples*, which was certainly not a formula likely to satisfy those who regarded Algeria as no more than a small part of the national territory. Similarly, *the loss of independence*, cited among the first consequences of State disintegration, suggests, in advance, the style as well as the content of a certain foreign policy" (p. 549).

We can, of course, study the events of May 13 as others
have often done, with close attention to the role, which was
considerable, of the intrigues and conspiracies of the French
rebels in Algiers, a minority of whom were Gaullist, though
not directed or even advised by the general. The latter, as
is his habit, took events as they came in order to put them
to the best possible use; considered what he knew or could
learn of the development of the Algerian situation in order
to determine his own course of action. According to the
historians of those troubled days, De Gaulle acted with skill,
weighed the words of each of his communiqués, scheduled
his press conference in the Palais d'Orsay three days in
advance, certain that, in the interval, events would enable
him to announce either the government's final impotence
(the most likely hypothesis) or his own temporary control
of affairs. But if, as I intend, we consider only General de
Gaulle's public declarations, there is no sign of an improvised, day-by-day tactic in his action. None of the sentences
he wrote or spoke at the time diverged from his perennial
insistence on respect for Republican institutions and on the
necessary State reform. De Gaulle dismisses the contingent
and the temporary. We discover, as the years go by, how
exactly he has been able to penetrate the nature of the
essential history that he discerns in the abundance and the
contradiction of daily events. The perspective we have now,
De Gaulle possessed then, gradually sifting a reality from
which he retained only the significant and lasting aspects.
Hence an analysis like the one I am attempting, limiting my
scrutiny to the general's texts, is as, if not more precise,
than those of the historians who are concerned with report-
ing the details of a policy elaborated from day to day, not
only according to General de Gaulle's words and acts, but
according to those of his adversaries or his colleagues.

On May 19, De Gaulle began the press conference that
was decisive in the disintegration not of the State (which
was, on the contrary, to be remade), but of the regime:

It will soon be three years since I last had the pleasure of seeing you. During our last meeting, I discussed with you my expectations, my apprehensions as to the course of events, and my determination to keep silence until, by breaking it, I could serve the nation. . . .

What is happening at this moment in Algeria in relation to metropolitan France, and in metropolitan France in relation to Algeria, can lead to an extremely grave national crisis. But it can also be the beginning of a kind of resurrection. That is why I believe this is the moment when I can be directly useful to France once again.

Useful, why? Because, in the past, certain things were accomplished, as the French know well, which the peoples associated with ours have not forgotten, and which other nations remember. In the face of the difficulties that assail us, the disasters that threaten, perhaps this moral capital will carry its weight in our policy at a moment of dangerous confusion.

Useful, too, because it is evident that the exclusive regime of the parties has not solved, is not solving, will not solve the enormous problems that face us, notably the association of France with the peoples of Africa, the coexistence of the various communities in Algeria, and even the problem of concord within each of these communities. . . .

Useful, finally, because I am but one man; because I am not identified with any party, any organization; because for six years I have taken no political action, for three years I have made no declaration—because I am a man who belongs to no one and who belongs to everyone.

Useful, how? Well, if the people so desire, as in the previous great national crisis, useful at the head of the government of the French Republic.

One man, a man who belongs to no one—that is the truth. A truth perhaps unique in history: to no one, not even to himself. He has no "career," he is beyond any ambition. To the question: "You have said you would be ready to assume the powers of the Republic. What do you mean by that?" De Gaulle replied:

The powers of the Republic, when one assumes them, can be only those the Republic itself will have delegated.

So much for the terms, which are perfectly clear. And then comes the man who has uttered them. The Republic! There was a time when it was denied, betrayed, by the parties themselves. Then I restored its arms, its laws, its name.

I waged war to attain victory for France, and I managed matters in such a way that it was a victory for the Republic as well. I did this with the cooperation of all, without exception, who were willing to join me in the undertaking. At their head, I re-established the Republic where it belongs. . . .

When all this was done, I gave the people their opportunity to speak, as I had promised. The people elected its representatives. To them I handed over, without any reservation or condition, the powers with which I had been entrusted.

And then, when I saw that the parties had reappeared like the émigrés of the past who had forgotten nothing and learned nothing, and that consequently it had become impossible for me to govern properly, then I withdrew, without seeking to force their hand in any way. Thereafter, they drew up a bad Constitution, despite me and against me.

I have not for a moment sought to violate that Constitution. In order to try to end confusion and to create a just and strong State, I instituted the Rassemblement du Peuple Français, appealing to a universal membership, without concern for origins, ideas, sentiments, or even labels. It so happened that the party regime managed to absorb, little by little, the officers of the Rassemblement, so that I no longer had the means of action within legality. At that time, I withdrew from public life.

This is how I have served and, apparently, threatened the Republic. Therefore when I hear—and this has gone on for eighteen years!—the professional saviors of the Republic, who would have been hard put to restore it by their own means, attributing to me the desire to attack public liberties, destroy the rights of the trade unions, demolish Republican institutions, I turn and pass on my way. Which does not keep me—along with many others, moreover—from asking these saviors what they have done with a liberated France and a restored Republic?

Which put matters in their place. And what was the answer? The general had right on his side, both in the field and on the blackboard. And clinically, upon the tortured body of the nation. But he was not right by force, he would finally be right because the people's instinct of self-preservation was in agreement with the will and the mind of General de Gaulle.

As for the accusation of fascism, it had indeed lasted for some eighteen years. As early as his Albert Hall speech of November 15, 1941, De Gaulle could say:

It is true that to the question: "What does Free France seek?" some, who have nothing to do with Free France, are often quick to answer in her place. Thus we have on occasion seen attributed to us, simultaneously, the most contradictory intentions, either by the enemy, or by that kind of friend who, doubtless out of zeal, cannot contain the alacrity of his suspicions in regard to us. One of the rare diversions granted by my present task is occasionally comparing these various assertions. For it is amusing to observe that the Free French are judged, on the same day, at the same hour, as inclining toward fascism, or preparing the restoration of a constitutional monarchy, or pursuing the integral re-establishment of the parliamentary Republic, or seeking to restore the prewar politicians, especially those of Jewish race or communist allegiance.

The insinuations of "that kind of friend who, doubtless out of zeal, cannot contain the alacrity of his suspicions in regard to us," were particularly tenacious in the accusations of anti-Republicanism. On April 1, 1942, De Gaulle, at the dinner of the National Defense Public Interest Committee, was led to say:

How, after this, can one attribute any importance to certain suggestions that the democracies should recognize France in the person of the men of Vichy rather than in that of the leaders of Fighting France, on the pretext that the latter have not taken a sufficiently clear position in favor of freedom! There is, in such an allegation, a veritable outrage to the democracies themselves,

for it attributes to them, in the first place, the intention of inter-
vening in what is exclusively the sovereignty of the French people. But it also imputes a comic blindness to the democracies.
For to prefer the men who have destroyed every French liberty
and who are attempting to model their regime on fascism or on
its caricature, rather than to trust those good Frenchmen who
persist in applying the laws of the Republic, who are locked in
a death struggle against the totalitarian enemy, who have clearly
stated their intention of delivering the captive nation in order to
revive its sovereignty—this would be, in truth, to introduce into
politics the principle of the wretched simpleton who flung himself into the sea for fear of getting wet.

This says a great deal about what De Gaulle was obliged
to endure at the time. Such accusations were no less painful being discreetly muffled. Thus when a reporter asked
him, during his May 27, 1942, press conference, whether he
was in favor of making the representation of the French
people, as it would be instituted after the war, "democratic,
republican, on the basis of universal suffrage," De Gaulle answered that "he himself and the overwhelming majority of
Frenchmen, whose opinion was known to him, were entirely
determined to recover national sovereignty and the republican form of government." The man who had asked the
question did not feel satisfied by this answer and retorted,
with all the insinuation these apparently anodyne words
could muster, that "there was an essential word in the question: the word *democratic.*" Patiently, calmly, De Gaulle
clarified:

Democracy is entirely identified, for me, with national sovereignty. Democracy means government of the people, by the people, and national sovereignty means the people exercising its
sovereignty unimpeded.

Such is his true thought, which the new Constitution has
made into a reality. De Gaulle, the sole revolutionary, is at
bottom the sole democrat, in the absolute sense of the word,

since he alone demands that the people decide without intermediary—and since it is this demand that makes him suspect in the eyes of the bourgeoisie of the Left, and that earns him their label of demagogue.

As for the accusation of fascism, the Allies hurled it as readily as our compatriots. In Beirut, on September 10, 1942, the general received Wendell Willkie, Roosevelt's Republican adversary in the November 1940 elections, now sent by him on a fact-finding mission. De Gaulle discusses the meeting in his *War Memoirs*:

In reference to me, he employed the standard malevolent banter in the book that appeared under his name upon his return. Because we had conferred together in the High Commissioner's office, which M. de Martel had recently provided with a suite of Empire furniture, Willkie represented me as aping the Napoleonic style; because I was wearing the standard officer's summer uniform of white linen, he saw an ostentatious parody of Louis XIV; and because one of my men spoke of "General de Gaulle's mission," Mr. Willkie hinted that I took myself for Joan of Arc. In this matter, Roosevelt's rival was also his imitator (II, p. 31).

It is still necessary to remind today's complaining friends and allies that from the very first they treated De Gaulle without the respect due him—and not only De Gaulle, but France—and that De Gaulle's crime, in their eyes, is to have made them liars by confronting them with a living France capable of saying "no."

This has lasted, then, some eighteen years. But it has grown more insistent during the past thirteen. Since the pathetic: "And I beg you to believe me" of July 29, 1945, to the words of May 19, 1958, whose calm irony does not conceal their bitterness, when he replied to a reporter who once again remarked, at the Palais d'Orsay: "There is some fear that if you return to power, you will abolish public liberties":

Have I ever done so? On the contrary, I re-established them when they disappeared. Does anyone believe that at sixty-seven I am going to begin a career as a dictator?

In the interval, from speech to speech, from city to city, from year to year, he always made the same answer, the same protest. He who was suspected of dictatorial ambitions, denounced dictatorship as a danger as early as the speech in Bayeux on June 16, 1946:

Indeed, the dissolution of the State has as its unavoidable consequence the dissatisfaction of the citizens with their institutions. At this point the mere existence of an opportunity creates the threat of a dictatorship, particularly since the more or less mechanical organization of modern society makes order in the control and functioning of the institutions more and more imperative, and more and more desired. How and why have the First, Second, and Third Republics come to an end in France? How and why did Italian democracy, the Weimar Republic, and the Spanish Republic give way to the regimes that followed them? . . . And yet, what is a dictatorship, except a tremendous risk? Doubtless its beginnings seem advantageous. Amid the enthusiasms of some and the resignation of the rest, in the rigor of the order it imposes, with the aid of striking accessories and a monolithic propaganda, it initially assumes a dynamic quality, which contrasts with the anarchy that preceded it. But it is the fate of a dictatorship to exaggerate its undertakings. . . . The nation becomes a machine which its master frantically accelerates. . . . Ultimately, the mainspring breaks. The imposing structure collapses in disaster and bloodshed. The nation is brought down lower than it was before the risk was taken.

If De Gaulle spoke this way, it was in answer less to his adversaries than to certain overeager friends who would encourage him to take that risk.

In Épinal, on September 29, 1946, he declared:

The pledge we made, we have purely and simply kept. As soon as it was possible, we called upon every Frenchman and every Frenchwoman to vote, in order to elect first the provisional municipal councils, then the general councils, and finally a National Assembly to which we immediately and without reservation handed over, as we had always promised, the powers we exercised for over five burdensome years. . . .

That is why—let it be said in passing—we respond with iron scorn to the absurd imputations of dictatorial ambitions that some, today, lavish upon us and that are exactly the same as the ineffectual taunts flung at us since June 18, 1940, by the enemy and his accomplices, by the mob of malcontent intriguers, and finally by certain foreign powers attacking, through our person, the independence of France and the integrity of her rights.

De Gaulle's hostility to dictatorship was derived not from a principle, a belief, but from the analysis of reality. He knew the recent history of Germany, Italy, Spain, and he knew his own people. This was enough to make him an old-style liberal, but one who finally, and by his own means, imposed his Constitution, his foreign policy, and everything he believed, even if he was the only man in France who believed it.

From speech to speech, from city to city, he developed the same theme. In Strasbourg, on April 7, 1947:

Victory attained and the nation consulted by means of elections, the parties have reappeared, impatient for their accession and in agreement on one point alone, that they be left a clear field. Under such conditions, and given the fact that I rejected the notion of any plebiscite—which, I am convinced, in the present state of the public mind and the present international situation, would ultimately lead to disastrous upheavals—there were, for the man speaking to you today, only two possible solutions. Either to play the parties' game—which would, I believe, have profitlessly diminished the kind of national capital that events have led him to represent, and thereby forced him to compromise on essentials; or else to let the parties conduct their experiment, having previously established the people's ability to determine, by means of referendum, the regime to be adopted. I have chosen this second solution.

In Paris, on April 27, 1947:

In June 1940, in the general collapse, when it was impossible
for the people to make themselves heard, it is entirely true that
I assumed and exercised power until I could restore it to the
national representation. Yes, I returned from Egypt and even
from Libya, from Italy, from the Rhine and the Danube, I entered Paris, Lyons, Marseilles, Rennes, Lille, Toulouse, Strasbourg, in the ranks of our victorious troops. And did I smother
the Republic? We must speak seriously about serious matters.
We must put an end to the exploitation of terms, which can
deceive only those who already wanted to be deceived.

In Paris, on February 11, 1950:

I could, of course, impose the institutions of my choice. But
you know my conviction that nothing solid, nothing lasting can
be created in France except on the basis of the will expressed by
the people. Had I transgressed that will, there would have been
a dictatorship—mine, of course. It cannot be doubted that the
latter would have sooner or later flung the nation into violent
upheaval. . . . In short, France would soon have found herself
in an impossible situation, both internally and externally. Yet
even had I been able to maintain control, after my regime, what
upheavals would have threatened the nation, what accession,
save that of communism? When a man holds the fate of a people
in his hands, he must look beyond himself. I have not accepted
the solution of dictatorship.

During the crisis of May 1958, De Gaulle said in his answer to M. Vincent Auriol:

The events in Algeria have been, as you know, provoked by
the chronic impotence of the government, which in the past I
have done everything within my power to remedy.

The upheaval and its subsequent developments have made use
of my name, without my having had anything to do with them.
Things being what they are, I have proposed to form, by legal
means, a government that I believe can restore unity, re-establish
discipline in the State, notably in the military realm, and promote
the national adoption of a reformed Constitution.

Now I encounter a determined opposition on the part of the national representation. On the other hand, I know that in Algeria and in the Army the tendency is such that, whatever I have said, whatever I say today, the failure of my proposal may drown all restraint and even overthrow the high command.

Since I cannot consent to receive power from any source other than the people, or at least its representatives (as I did in 1944 and 1945), I fear that we are heading for anarchy and civil war.

And, on the night of June 3, he wearily, but with the same irony, offered this last clarification to the deputies:

I confess I am somewhat surprised to learn that there can be any ambiguity between us on the subject of the existence or non-existence of an Assembly elected by universal suffrage, or on the ultimate identification of the functions of the President of the Republic with those of the head of the government.

This seems to me so contradictory to the lifelong experience of the members of the government, to common sense, and finally to the existence of the Republic itself, that I am astonished that the question can be raised. In any case, as far as I am concerned, I am not at all embarrassed to say what I think, it being clearly understood that the draft that will be submitted to the referendum will not be my own but the work of the government, assisted by the committee established for this draft.

No, what will happen will be the continuation of the Republic, for you must understand that if I have made the government I have, I have made it so that the Republic may continue!

Lastly, as for my opinion about the necessity of an Assembly elected by universal suffrage, one that will, moreover, be the chief Assembly in tomorrow's Parliament, I shall give you a further, final proof: that proof is the pleasure and the honor I feel at being among you this evening.

"Once again at the rendezvous of the Republic and at the rendezvous of History" (this is how André Malraux introduced him), De Gaulle, in his speech of September 4, 1958, in the Place de la République, once again answered the same accusations:

What had to be done *has been done* in order to obviate the irremediable at the very moment it was about to occur. The rending of the nation was prevented just in time. The ultimate opportunity of the Republic has been safeguarded. It is with legality that I and my government have assumed the exceptional mandate of establishing a draft for a new Constitution and of submitting it to the decision of the people.

We have done so on the basis of principles defined at the time of our investiture. We have done so with the collaboration of the consultative council instituted by law. We have taken into account the formal advice of the Council of State. We have done so after very free and searching deliberations among our own ministerial councils, formed of men as various as possible in origin and tendencies, but resolutely united. We have done so without violating any right of the people or any public liberty. The nation, which alone may judge, will approve or reject our work, which we offer it in all conscience.

What patience! He has consented to be suspected and denounced by the most tractable Leftists, like Guy Mollet and Lacoste, who would provide the most effective agents for an activist policy of the Right.

In this same speech, De Gaulle presented the draft of the Constitution to which the nation had to answer, on September 28, yes or no:

It is, then, for the people we are, in the age and the world we live in, that the draft of the Constitution has been prepared, so that the nation may be effectively directed by those whom it chooses and to whom it grants the trust that is the basis of legitimacy.

So that, above the political conflict, there will exist a national arbiter, elected by citizens who possess a public mandate, an arbiter responsible for ensuring the regular functioning of institutions; empowered to resort to the judgment of the sovereign people; answering, in case of extreme danger, for the independence, the honor, the integrity of France and for the safety of the Republic. So that a government will exist that is created to govern, that is given the time and the possibility to do so, that is not deflected from its task, and that, thereby, deserves the nation's adherence. So that a Parliament exists to represent the nation's political will, to vote on the laws, to control the executive power without having to exceed its role. So that the government and the Parliament will collaborate but remain separate as to their responsibilities, and so that no member of the one may, at the same time, be a member of the other. Such is the balanced structure which the public powers must assume. The rest will depend on men.

Having finally prevailed, De Gaulle, after the referendum of September 28, 1958, in his October 23 press conference addressed "tomorrow's Parliament" in terms close to those in which he had warned the Parliaments of yesterday:

After some months of suspension, the parliamentary institution is about to reappear, but it will no longer be omnipotent. The lesson taught by facts, the course of events, the judgment of the public, and the civic spirit of the French political body as a whole have led the constituents of 1958—that is, the members of the government, aided by the labors of the Constitutional Council, the advice of the Council of State, and, I must say, by the enlightened advice of the President of the Republic, to establish specific limits and powerful controls for future Assemblies. The nation has ratified their work. This is, in effect, the present situation: the necessities of national recovery absolutely forbid us to return to yesterday's confusion.

If by some misfortune it were to happen that tomorrow's Parliament should refuse to abide by the role that has devolved upon it, there is no doubt that the Republic would be flung into a new crisis whose outcome no one can foresee, except that the parliamentary institution itself would certainly be swept away for a long time. . . .

In a word, it is by profoundly reforming the representative system that we have preserved its chances. May these chances be kept from destroying themselves!

On December 21, 1958, General de Gaulle was elected President of the Republic. He received 78.5 per cent of the votes. On January 8, 1959, he officially assumed his functions at the Élysée. M. René Cassin, Vice President of the Council of State, announced the results of the election. His first words were:

To President René Coty, who himself received the homage of the public officials on December 23, belongs the honor of welcoming to the Élysée, in your person, the great citizen elected, by a free referendum, President of the Republic and of the French Community.

And his last:

Monsieur le Président, I shall not evoke the personal memory of those hours when the young General de Gaulle read his first appeal to the Resistance and assumed at great risk, with a faith shared at first by a small number of comrades, then by the entire people, the direction of the supreme interests of the nation, while preparing the restoration of its free institutions.

But let me at least be permitted to remark, in the name of the college made up of the leaders of the highest French jurisdiction, that your election to the position of supreme responsibility has been accomplished under the aegis of independent magistrates and with respect for the law. A true democracy requires not only that those who wield authority accept the correlative responsibilities, but also that the primacy of the law be placed in the safekeeping of justice. Those who know how, in the most crucial moments, you have led the boldest actions with complete respect for institutions and for pledges, have confidence that under your seven-year term the Republic will not simply continue and prosper with rejuvenated vigor and structures, but that it will retain for France the human countenance haloed with noble prestige that has won her the affection of nations and particularly those of our brothers in the member States of the French Community.

Thus the Vice President of the Council of State formally underlined General de Gaulle's constant concern since 1940 to remain within Republican legality.

M. René Coty declared:

For the first time in our country, a revolution—a necessary revolution, a constructive revolution—has been effected with calm hearts, cool heads, and respect for the very laws that are to be reformed.

It is the Parliament of the Fourth Republic that has legally entrusted the government with the mandate to propose a new Constitution to the sovereign people, who, by an overwhelming majority, have made it the Constitution of France.

This unification [*rassemblement*] of the citizens of old France and of the French Community, whatever may have been, whatever may still be, their differences, finds its conclusion in this presidential election whose electors were for the most part the departmental and communal elected officers of the Fourth Republic.

Thus liberty has been in a position to call upon the authority that alone can effectively defend and guarantee it.

Thus, as I told you when I greeted you for the first time in this palace, the conjunction of what Pascal called "greatness of establishment" with what, with him, we call "personal greatness" has been duly effected.

There remains for me, Monsieur le Président, the privilege of thanking you once again, in the name of the Republic, for having assumed even in its most ungrateful tasks the weighty and great mission of the recovery of the State.

The last President of the Fourth Republic acknowledged in a sense that the *rassemblement*, thanks to De Gaulle, had finally been effected and that it had triumphed. In his answer, the new President of the Republic deliberately emphasized the formality of this transmission of power:

I am profoundly sensitive to all that is imposing and moving in this ceremony.

Your words, Monsieur le Président, whose wisdom is all the more striking for being spoken by a great citizen leaving with perfect dignity the mandate he has exercised in a truly exemplary manner; the formal proclamation of the election of December 21; the noble address of the President of the Constitutional Committee; the presence of the government, of the Dean and of one of the members of the Diplomatic Corps, of the Presidents and the Committees of the Senate, of the National Assembly and of the Economic Council, of the Prime Ministers of the new and young States of the French Community, of a marshal of France, of the High Chancellor of the Legion of Honor, of the Chancellor of the Order of the Liberation, of the representatives of all the bodies and services of the State and of the high command, of the delegation of the Académie française and of the Institut de France, all these confer upon our meeting the majestic character suitable to its subject.

Thus the renovated institutions of the French Republic and the new institutions of the French Community take effect. Thus the man to whom the former and the latter have, once again, delegated the responsibility of leading them to their destinies assumes his functions.

In the course of this ceremony on January 8, 1959, in which he officially took over his functions as President of the Republic, De Gaulle predicted the circumstances—which were in fact to occur—in which he would again have to deal with grave events. The last sentences of his address testify to this, imbued though they may seem to be with optimism and hope:

It is once again, as before, my duty to represent, to further, even, if the public safety should require it, to impose national interest in the nation, common interest in the larger Community.

These are my obligations. I shall live up to them, I can testify to that in advance. But to do so, I must have the co-operation of those who serve the Republic, the support of the men who are henceforth the leaders in Africa, the support of the French people and of the populations overseas. This support, this co-operation were once given to me in the anguish of national danger; I ask for them now when the horizon brightens with the light of our high hopes.

During his message to Parliament, on January 15, 1959, De Gaulle said:

When, eighteen years ago, the country was gasping in the anguish of its disaster, this recovery was no more than a dream. Today it has begun in earnest. But before it can be achieved, everyone must see that a rigorous ordering of our affairs is absolutely necessary in every domain in which our national destiny is at stake: the pacification and transformation of Algeria, which are, obviously, the indispensable conditions for a political solution, which can come only from universal suffrage; establishment of the French Community; France's renewed status in her alliances and in the role she plays in the world; modernization of our means of national defense; finances, exchanges, economy, currency; social, cultural, scientific progress.

This great goal will certainly be approved by the Assemblies. But to achieve it, many efforts are required from various French elements. This will be—as everyone knows—the decisive test of the Parliament. If by misfortune—which I myself do not envisage —the Parliament should yield to fractional promptings instead of identifying itself with the national welfare, the crisis of our institutions will recur. On the contrary, if, as I believe it will, the Parliament does not permit the trees of private interests, partisan rivalries, and local issues, to conceal the forest of French unity, then a great future is assured to our new Republic, and by it to the nation.

De Gaulle had addressed this warning, in almost the same terms, to the Parliament in his press conference of the previous September 23, and also, as we have seen, in the remote days of January 1946, when he was about to withdraw —for a long time—from the government and, it will be recalled, adjured the members of the Constituent Assembly: "We have begun to reconstruct the Republic. You will continue to do so. In whatever fashion you proceed . . . I believe I can tell you in all conscience that if you do so without taking into account the lessons of the past fifty years of our political history, and in particular of the events of 1940, if you do not take into account the absolute necessity that the government have authority, dignity, and responsibility, you will find yourselves in a situation such that, one day or another, I predict, you will bitterly regret having followed the course you have taken."

In his press conference on April 11, 1961, the general elaborated:

Actually, it is essential that the State possess, among its powers, the continuity and the authority without which, as is obvious, everything falls to rack and ruin in our country and in our difficult age. This implies that a head of State who has the nation's confidence answer, in the last resort, for what is essential and permanent in the imperiled life of France; that he not be identified with the many and episodic disputes that our natural divisions invariably introduce into our political life; that he possess the means necessary to enable the public powers to function regularly; that he be able, in certain cases, to call upon the nation to declare itself; and finally that in a grave crisis he be able to answer for France and for the Republic. . . .

It is clear that the way in which our institutions work bears the mark of the men and the circumstances of the moment. I do not deny, for example, that the fact I hold the office I do has several consequences, and I believe that our situation in regard to Africa, to Algeria, to the rest of the world, as well as the enormous changes we must effect within the French nation itself, do not fail to have their effects. In every period, human contingencies and the facts of the moment have counted and invariably will count for a great deal in the functioning of institutions, without necessarily jeopardizing principles or invalidating texts. But what is essential, what is for France an absolute necessity, is that in the historic period through which we are living France's government have a leader and also that the head of State possess that profound adherence in the nation that is indispensable to him if he is to fulfill his mission.

At the time of this same press conference of April 11, 1961, De Gaulle gave a glimpse of an ultimate and important modification in the Constitution, in regard to the election of the President of the Republic:

I know that many consider the method of electing the President of the Republic by an electoral college limited to only the elected officers—as it is composed according to the present text —will correspond poorly, for the man who succeeds me, to the popular and national mandate appropriate to the office, which was conferred upon me, exclusive of any election, by exceptional events—events that will, of course, not recur, or at least are not obliged to. I acknowledge, for my part, that there is indeed something inadequate about this method of designating the leader of the State who is to succeed me. In order to remedy this, by reinforcing, if I may use the expression, "the personal equation" of the future President, it may be that the nation should select him by universal suffrage. This could be considered. If it becomes necessary to replace me before there has been time to solve this problem, it will be up to those who are here when I am not to take the desired initiative. But if I myself have the time and the occasion, I can, at the proper moment, put on the agenda this point, which is so important for the future of France.

Thus, according to De Gaulle, the "popular and national mandate" indispensable to his office was granted him "by exceptional events, exclusive of any election."

A few days later, the Algiers putsch occurred. On April 23, De Gaulle addressed a message to the nation which concluded as follows:

The future of the usurpers must be what—and only what—the rigor of the laws makes inevitable.

Facing the disaster that hovers over the nation and the threat that weighs upon the Republic, having officially consulted the Constitutional Council, the Prime Minister, the President of the Senate, and the President of the National Assembly, I have decided to put in force Article 16 of our Constitution. As of today, I shall take, as needed, the measures that seem to me required by the circumstances. Thereby, I declare myself to be, today and tomorrow, within the French and Republican legitimacy that the nation has conferred upon me, which I shall maintain, whatever happens, until the conclusion of my mandate or until I lose either my strength or my life, and whose survival I shall take measures to ensure after my disappearance.

When asked, on May 15, 1962, if he would put the election of the President of the Republic by universal suffrage on the agenda, De Gaulle answered:

I spoke a word about this matter last year; my reply today is that I shall not do so for the moment. Let me add something to this subject, since I have the pleasure of seeing you and speaking to you, and since we are considering so prevalent an idea—I mean, what will happen when De Gaulle is no longer here. Well, I can tell you this much, which will perhaps explain in what direction we shall proceed in this regard: what is to be feared, to my mind, after the event to which I refer, is not a political void, but rather a political surfeit.

On September 20, 1962, he begins his televised address as follows:

Since the French people have called upon me to resume my place officially at their head, I, of course, feel obliged eventually to ask them a question that relates to my succession; I refer to the method of electing the chief of State. Reasons familiar to all of you have recently led me to believe that there might still be time in which to do this.

This allusion was understood readily enough on September 20, 1962. De Gaulle was to be more precise in his three subsequent speeches. On October 4:

First of all, the attacks perpetrated or prepared against my life make it an obligation for me to ensure, as far as I can, the succession of a strong Republic, which implies that it be so at the summit. Further, in the face of the general anxiety provoked by these attempted murders, anxiety as to the risks of public confusion France may suddenly run, I believe it is necessary that a massive vote of the nation attest, at this very moment, that it has institutions, that it intends to maintain them, and that it refuses, after De Gaulle, to see the State once again a victim of political practices that would lead to an odious catastrophe.

On October 18:

As proof is thus given of the value of a Constitution that calls for the State to have a leader, and as, even since I have filled this role, it has been apparent that the President of the Republic exists for no other reason, I believe in all conscience that the French people must now seal by a solemn vote its desire that this be the case today, tomorrow, and in the future. I believe that this is, for our people, the moment to decide the fact; otherwise, the attacks that have been perpetrated and those that are being prepared make it evident that my disappearance risks plunging France once again into the confusion of the past and, hard upon it, into catastrophe.

On October 26:

The question is to determine if, after me—and no one is unaware of the threats that weigh upon my life—the future Presidents will in their turn have, thanks to the direct investiture of the nation, the means and the obligation to bear this burden, heavy as it is. In short, the question is to indicate by a formal ballot that, whatever happens, the Republic will continue, in the form we have determined by an overwhelming majority.

This is typically De Gaulle: he is neither surprised nor outraged by the attacks. He spares us even the slightest sign of reprobation. He remarks on the risk and plans first of all to utilize it for the fulfillment of a great design: the election of the President of the Republic by universal suffrage. Thanks to the murderers, the operation has become a simple one. Bastien-Thiry has played into the Gaullist hand —such is the fate of all of De Gaulle's adversaries. How he has used them! To the point where some of them (notably Giraud) have assumed almost a comic aspect in history.

Four speeches, then, in which he repeated himself in order to be certain that he was clearly understood in the few days that preceded the referendum. We notice, in the speech of September 20, the words "since the French people have called upon me to resume my place officially at their head," which imply that *unofficially* De Gaulle never stopped feeling responsible for France. Another adverb—*implicitly*—indicated the same certainty on October 4:

But, in order to be, vis-à-vis himself and vis-à-vis the others, in a position to fulfill such a mission, the President needs the nation's direct confidence. Instead of possessing it implicitly, as was my own case in 1958 for historic and exceptional reasons that could justify, at the outset, the limited College (whose vote I am certainly not forgetting!), it is henceforth essential that the President be elected by universal suffrage.

After a glance at the recent past (the adoption, by 80 per cent of the voters, of a Constitution that has "given its proofs"), after reminding his audience that the President of the Republic henceforth answers for France and for the Republic, that he must "inspire, direct, and orient the national action," and even that he may have to lead that action directly—"as I have done, for example, in the entire Algerian affair"—in short, after insisting on the fact that one "of the essential characteristics of the Constitution of the Fifth Republic is that it gives the State a leader," De Gaulle added in the most important of these addresses:

However, for the President of the Republic to be able to exercise such a responsibility effectively, he must have the nation's explicit confidence. Permit me to say that in resuming my place at the head of the State in 1958, I believed that in this regard, the events of history had already done what was necessary for me. By virtue of what we have lived through and learned together, through so much blood and suffering, but also with so much hope, enthusiasm, and success, there exists between you, Frenchmen, Frenchwomen, and myself an exceptional link that invests and binds me. I therefore did not attach a particular importance at the time to the method by which I assumed office, since my position was established in advance by the pressure of events. Further, taking into account certain political susceptibilities, some of which were quite respectable, I chose, at that moment, to avoid a formal plebiscite in my behalf. In short, I accepted at the time the initial text of our Constitution which submits the election of the President to a relatively limited College of about eighty thousand members.

But if this method of balloting could no more than any other determine my responsibilities in regard to France, or by itself express the confidence the French seek to place in me, the question becomes different for those who will succeed me, one after the other, in the position I occupy at present, without having necessarily received from events the same national identification. For these men to be in a position, and fully obliged, to bear the supreme responsibility, whatever its weight, and thus for our Republic to have every likelihood of remaining strong, effective, and genuinely national despite the demons of our divisions, they must receive their mission directly from the whole body of citizens (September 20, 1962).

As a result of this, De Gaulle believed he owed the nation the following proposal: "When my own seven-year term is over, or if death or disease should interrupt it beforehand, the President of the Republic will henceforth be elected by universal suffrage." A decision justified in terms that exceed strict reason, without, however, being contestable. If the general, speaking of himself, often says: "De Gaulle," this is because he regards himself from outside, in the timeless light of history. The balloting by which he was elected President of the Republic could *not more than any other*, determine his responsibilities in regard to France. He knows for himself his duties as well as his rights: he is *bound*. In this calm pride, we detect two traces of a quite formal prudence: he says he received national identification from *events*, without reminding his audience that these events were created by him in his action of June 18; he adds that his successors will not *necessarily* benefit from such events, which is a way of suggesting that there is little likelihood that the conditions of such a consecration will recur. On October 4, he repeated: "Since I took office in answer to

the nation's appeal the method of electing the President
was at the start secondary, since the role was filled. But
today the question is a crucial one." And on October 18:
". . . Increasingly aware, as I am, of the historic responsibility incumbent upon me in regard to the nation, I ask
you, quite simply, to determine that henceforth you will
elect your President by universal suffrage."

De Gaulle represents, he *is* the nation without the latter
needing to confirm him in this identification which it has
acknowledged once and for all. That is why election by
universal suffrage, which he considers it necessary to establish for his successors, is not necessary for him. Further,
although he was elected, according to the Constitution then
in effect, by a limited College, the general regards himself
as possessing a direct mandate from the nation.

In these televised addresses of September 20 and October
4, 18, and 26, 1962, De Gaulle, after reviewing the conditions under which, in 1958, he "again assumed responsibility for the destiny of the nation"; after emphasizing that
the new Constitution has rejected "the confusion and the
impotence of the former regime, that is, the exclusive regime of the parties" and thus corresponds to the "conditions
that the abrupt and rapid life of the modern world imposes
on a great State"; after showing the "brilliant progress" that
has resulted for the nation, amid the difficulties of a decolonization that could not have been effected without this
reform; after repeating that "the continuity, the strength,
the effectiveness of the State, instituted at the summit, are
the necessary conditions of the renovation that we have
begun, which inspires our young people and which astounds
the world"; De Gaulle asked the people to determine that
henceforth the President of the Republic would be elected
by universal suffrage and added:

Naturally, all the old political parties, whose blindness nothing
that has occurred could cure, urge you to answer "No!" This is

quite natural on their part. For it is true that today my action at the head of the Republic, and tomorrow that of the successive Presidents who will be invested by the confidence of the people and who will be able, if necessary, to ask for its sovereign verdict, is incompatible with the absolute and disastrous reign of the parties.

After the sovereign decision made by the nation on October 28, 1962, enacting a constitutional law that "henceforth the French people will elect their President by universal suffrage," De Gaulle, in his televised address of November 7, again attacked the parties he once more found leagued against him:

But also the referendum has illuminated once more, a fundamental political fact of our time: the parties of the past, even when a common professional passion momentarily unites them, do not represent the nation. This was clearly and terribly evident when, in 1940, their regime abdicated amid the disaster. It was apparent once again in 1958, when their regime on the brink of anarchy, collapse, and civil war, appealed to me. It has just been verified in 1962.

What has happened, in effect? The nation being vigorous, the treasuries full, the franc stronger than ever, decolonization completed, the Algerian drama over, the army entirely under discipline again, French prestige restored to its highest point throughout the world, in short, all immediate danger averted and the situation of France well established both internally and externally, we saw all the parties of the past turn against De Gaulle. We saw them all oppose the referendum because it tended to prevent their regime from beginning again. In order to keep the government at their mercy once again, and to return as soon as possible to the intrigues that were their pleasure but that will be the ruin of France, we saw them unite, without a single abstention, first in the Parliament to censure the Ministry, then before the nation to induce it to answer "No" to me. Yet now we see that their united force has just been disavowed by the French people.

After admitting that the "parties of the past espouse and still serve various currents of opinion," and recalling "that throughout the war years and the years of peace in which he directed the nation's affairs, he has, according to his opportunities, chosen his ministers from all political groups, alternately and without exception," De Gaulle came (the elections being scheduled for the following November 18 and 25), to the future Parliament:

But it is a fact that to identify the parties of the past with France and the Republic today would be simply ridiculous.

Indeed, by voting "Yes" outside of and despite the parties, the nation has just approved a broad policy of political renewal. I say that it is altogether necessary, if our democracy is to endure, that this policy be strengthened and enlarged and, first of all, that it be established by a majority in the Parliament. If, in fact, the Parliament, which possesses the legislative and veto power, were to reappear, tomorrow, dominated by the factions so familiar to us, the factions determined to re-establish their former impotent rule, contradicting the profound desire the nation has just expressed, then such a Parliament, having a less truly representative character than ever and, moreover, divided into rival and opposing groups, would, from the very first, be victimized by every kind of obstruction, ultimately plunging the public powers into an all too familiar confusion, until, sooner or later, it caused the State to founder in a new national crisis.

And De Gaulle besought the French:

Ah, decide so that this second referendum does not nullify the first! Despite all local issues, all fragmentary considerations, confirm by the selection of men the choice you have made for our destiny by voting "Yes" in the referendum!

Frenchmen, Frenchwomen, I ask this of you! I ask it of you, with an eye to matters far beyond my own person and my own present office. I ask it of you once again, on the grounds—the only ones that matter to me—of the good of the State, the fate of the Republic, and the future of France.

Often De Gaulle had used stinging phrases from the RPF days when he alluded sarcastically to the "faction of mediocrity, which is also that of chloroform" (May 1, 1949), to the scornful and famous formulas of the years of his return to power: "As a result each eddy brings into action the various factions of peevishness, resentment, and spleen [harge, grogne, et rogne]" (July 12, 1961). ". . . One sometimes smells in the air certain attempts to demoralize the public. But all this is merely the scum floating on top of the depths" (September 5, 1961). "But if, by some mischance, we were once again to allow the troublemakers, the tumult, the incoherence that we know so well, to take possession of our undertakings, abasement would be our fate" (October 2, 1961). Never, though, had he carried sarcasm so far as in this speech of November 7, 1962. This was because the parties, which he might have supposed defeated, had once again tried to oppose his action, those "parties of the past" whose regime, after having "abdicated amid the disaster" had *appealed to him on the brink of the abyss*. But this time they would have to disappear: the elections of November 1962 brought to the French Parliament for the first time in our history a majority that could protect De Gaulle from any future distraction from his policy by the demands of politics.

Because he has seen so clear-sightedly in the past, De Gaulle, free henceforth to manage our future, does so with a determination and an assurance that are unfailingly impressive. And he alludes to this past, not without pride, to disarm the objections or protests his atomic policy provokes. He declared, for example, on April 19, 1963:

In short, our nation, perpetually threatened, finds itself once again confronted with the necessity of possessing the most powerful weapons of the age, unless, of course, the other nations cease to possess them. However, in order to dissuade us from this course, the simultaneous voices of immobilism and demagoguery are, as always, raised. "It is no use!" say some. "It is too expensive!" say others. These voices France has heeded in the past, to her cost, notably on the eve of each of the two World Wars. "No heavy artillery!" they shouted in unison until 1914. "No armored

corps! No attack planes!" the same groups of blind and backward
minds exclaimed in chorus. But this time we shall not permit
routine and illusion to bring invasion upon us. And now, amid
the strained and dangerous world in which we live, our principal
duty is to be strong and to be ourselves.

France "has institutions, she intends to maintain them."
She seeks to have them "remain what they are, today, tomorrow, and in the future." The press conference of January 31, 1964, in places resembles almost word for word that
of April 11, 1960, which already had as its theme: "Our
Constitution is functioning." The "I do not deny that the
fact I hold the office I do has several consequences . . ." of
April 11, 1960, corresponds to these words of January 31,
1964: "As for the President, it is true that his personal
equation has counted, but I do not doubt that, from the
beginning, this was anticipated." The expression "personal
equation" was moreover used by the general in the press
conference of April 11, 1960, when he raised the possibility
of electing the President of the Republic by universal suffrage, in order to reinforce his "personal equation."

The grave crisis—again anticipated, on April 11, 1960—
exploded a few days later with the putsch of April 22. This
was why De Gaulle could declare on January 31, 1964:

It must also be said that our institutions have had to function,
for over five years, in very variable conditions, including at certain moments the pressure of grave attempts at subversion. But
the test of men and of circumstances has shown precisely that
the instrument corresponds to its object, not only in regard to
the ordinary process of events, but even in regard to difficult
situations which the present Constitution, as we have seen, affords us the means to confront: See Article 16, dissolution of the
National Assembly.

No doubt this success is derived essentially from the fact that
our new institutions correspond to the demands of the times as
well as to the nature of the French people and what that people

truly desires. Yet some, finding the bride too beautiful, as we say, are suggesting changes that, in fact, would overthrow the entire system.

The Constitution, as it functions today, does not seem to De Gaulle to require improvement except in points of detail:

The spirit of the new Constitution, while maintaining a legislative Parliament, consists of keeping power out of the hands of the parties and allowing it to come directly from the people, which implies that the head of State, elected by the nation, be its source and possessor. This is what was achieved, as everyone acknowledged, first when I resumed the direction of the affairs of State, then when I assumed the office of President of the Republic. This is what the last referendum has simply emphasized. Since it has been in effect, this conception does not seem to have been misconstrued by those in positions of power, rejected by the people, or invalidated by events.

Declaring that for the present and for the future, except for changes in style, President of the Republic, whoever he may be, is the only possessor of the indivisible authority of the State, De Gaulle, on January 31, 1964, extended further than ever before his conception of the powers attributed to himself and his successors:

In effect, the President who, according to our Constitution, is the man the nation has instituted in office to answer for its destiny; the President, who chooses the Prime Minister, who appoints him as well as the other members of the government, who has the power to change him, either because his task is accomplished or because the President no longer approves of him; the President, who formulates the decisions made in the councils, promulgates the laws, negotiates and signs the treaties, ratifies—or refuses to ratify—the measures proposed to him, who is the head of the armies, who appoints to public office; the President, who in case of danger must take it upon himself to do all that is necessary; this President is obviously the only man to possess and to delegate the authority of the State . . .

But although it must be understood that the indivisible authority of the State is entirely entrusted to the President by the people who have elected him; that there is no other power—neither ministerial, nor civil, nor military, nor judiciary—that is not conferred and maintained by him; and lastly that it is his responsibility to co-ordinate his own supreme power with the powers whose direction he assigns to others, nevertheless everything obliges the maintenance, in ordinary times, of the distinction between the function and the field of action of the head of State and those of the Prime Minister.

This De Gaulle has always believed, if he has never said it so clearly before. But these are remarks reaffirmed in all the essentials a thousand times. The impression that we have already heard, already seen these things before is one we constantly experience in studying General de Gaulle's thought and action in one circumstance or another in which he seems to be repeating the same words, the same gestures. Chronology vanishes, time becomes indistinguishable, events pass, De Gaulle appears, withdraws, returns, remains—unchanged.

The consistency of the general's thought, in regard to Constitutional problems is evidenced by the texts we have assembled, even as the history of these recent years reminds us that De Gaulle was obliged, without sacrificing anything of his desire for reform, to adapt it, nonetheless, to necessities that he had not been able to anticipate but that, with his habitual realism, his empiricism, he has been able to take into account. What, for De Gaulle, must be beyond any possibility of corruption, what must be immutable, is not so much the Constitution (even though this was his own work) as what it is responsible for maintaining in its integrity: the State.

In his declaration concerning Algeria of October 23, 1958, which we shall quote below, the general appealed to "the nature of things." If he made important changes in his Constitution of 1958, this was, as he himself indicated on September 5, 1960, because "the nature of things is stronger than constitutional texts." It matters little that our country has had seventeen Constitutions in one hundred and fifty years, if France continues. The ideal Constitution being an impossibility, other adaptations, other evolutions, perhaps other revolutions will be necessary. At most, we may hope that the reforms, imposed by experience, that De Gaulle effected in the organization of the public powers will hold on this essential point: the necessity for the State to have a leader. And that in this way we may surmount, in so far as is possible, the difficulty Paul Valéry expressed in these words: "If the State is strong, it crushes us. If it is weak, we perish."

III

ETERNAL FRANCE—the phrase is wartime rhetoric, but permanent France is a reality, as a permanent Germany, a permanent England are realities. That is what De Gaulle knows because that is what he sees. Europe does not exist in his mind as an idea, or as a dream. It is being created before his eyes, and he watches it being created, and he helps it into being, not according to the model he has in his mind, but according to the possibilities reality proposes and taking into account the clues of history.

Europe will never be a corporation. Perhaps it will ultimately constitute a true family, that is, a tangled knot of convergent or contradictory interests and of passions bequeathed from a bloody past. Each member of this illustrious family has his own genius, and hence his individual vocation. What they have in common is a will to persist as they are, a will that has made them all capable, at certain periods, of the worst follies in every realm (like so many individual human beings . . .). The difference here between an individual and a nation is that age weakens and disarms men; the nations do not grow old.

The nations do not grow old: it is as if the nations emerged from the blood baths and the baths of mud—fortified. Germany, bisected after two wars lost, her finest cities destroyed, Germany seethes with power and vitality. But perhaps she has learned—perhaps!—to mistrust herself at last. She has dared to face the consequences of her madness. She has drawn closer to us for the first time without a secret motive of domination. And we, "scoured" by De Gaulle, we see ourselves, judge ourselves as we are, reduced to our exact proportions, too weak ever to become again the insatiable great nation of Louis XIV, of the First Republic, and of the Empire.

But there is no reason for me to speculate further about Europe, about Germany, and about what General de Gaulle thinks of them, for he has never, during the past twenty years, failed to speak his mind on these subjects. Let us turn back to the sources.

On March 18, 1944, in Algiers, when a mortally wounded Germany still remained in the battle, and when France, in the eyes of President Roosevelt, was entirely a thing of the past, her destiny "finished," De Gaulle showed us when we were scarcely out of the abyss into which we had been cast, in a few incandescent phrases what his allies did not see and what he did see: what Europe would be, at the moment of her rebirth, and what the place of France would be within that Europe:

And yet, Europe exists, conscious of her value in the whole of humanity, certain of emerging from the sea of her sufferings, of reappearing, enlightened by her ordeals and ready to undertake, for the organization of the world, that constructive labor—material, intellectual, moral—of which she is eminently capable, once the capital cause of her miseries and her divisions, the frenzied power of Prussianized Germanism has been torn from her breast. Then the action, the influence and, indeed, the value of France will be, as history, geography, and common sense command, essential to Europe in orienting and linking that continent to the world. In attitude and policy the government is doing its best to prepare, even in the combat, the European role that France will be able to play tomorrow for the advantage of all.

De Gaulle was to evoke Europe two years later, on July 28, 1946, in Bar-le-Duc:

What then, if not the old world, can re-establish the equilibrium between the two new ones? The old Europe that for so many centuries was the guide of the universe is in a position to constitute the necessary element of compensation and comprehension at the heart of a world tending to split in two. The nations of the ancient West, which have for their vital arteries the North Sea, the Mediterranean, the Rhine, geographically situated between the two new masses, determined to maintain an independence that would be dangerously exposed in case of a conflagration, physically and morally linked to the massive effort of the Russians, as well as to the liberal impulse of the Americans, strong in their own resources and those of the vast territories allied to their destiny, spreading their influence and activity far and wide—what weight they would carry if they succeeded in combining their policies, despite the grievances exchanged from age to age!

Here then was the obvious truth stated in 1946 by this supposed adversary of Europe, though he has been the adversary only of a fictitious Europe created by those blind enough to believe that the whole can be of a different essence than the elements that compose it. As for De Gaulle, he can speak only in the name of France, but does not fail to do so.

Before Europe can be created, she must be defended as she stands, and she will not be defended without the cooperation of an independent and responsible France. On April 16, 1948, General de Gaulle announced his position at the first session of the Rassemblement in Marseilles:

We regard as criminal a policy and a strategy that, on the pretext that overwhelming atomic bombs already exist in other countries, would deliberately abandon the soil of metropolitan France, first to invasion, then to bombardment.

Certainly the means of France have narrow limits. But, as he said on May 1, 1949, "I have faced, with you, vastly narrower means without giving way to despair":

During the five years after the disaster and until the victory in which our war effort was pursued under the worst possible circumstances, do you suppose that I myself, our ministers, our fighting men were not often agonized by our penury in comparison to what French armies had been in other days? And yet the share taken in the battle by the forces we had trained in the Empire and in the interior, forces we engaged at the right time and in the right place, contributed greatly to the ultimate victory.

During his press conference of October 1, 1948, De Gaulle declared that there was "something inadequate in the attempt to organize in and around London the defense of Europe, which is above all a continent":

I believe that we must defend Europe in Europe, and I believe that by virtue of geography, history, and also psychology, Europe cannot be defended in London. . . . This is a question we will have to take up again, when France has an official policy and means, for in the preparation of a possible war, France must be the center of the strength and strategy of Western Europe.

Apropos of the Atlantic Pact, he said on March 29, 1949:

I have read that the Pact extends only to the North Atlantic, which suggests potentially serious disadvantages for the strategic preparation of the common effort. Further, if the Pact which extends to the North Atlantic covers Algeria, why does it fail to cover either Morocco or Tunisia? This is rather difficult to explain, except perhaps by motives that it would be better to dismiss from the minds of the signers.

And he repeated on November 14, 1949:

As for the defense of Europe, a kind of organization seems to be appearing whose name is not too often spoken, but whose nature I do not regard with favor. I do not believe that centering the defense of Europe in England is a good solution. . . .

It is inadmissible that French national defense and the direction of the French military effort be assumed by anyone but a Frenchman. That would be intolerable. From the moment the defense of our territory is in question, only the French can be responsible. What is being covertly concocted, I regard as highly disturbing. Indeed, what would be the meaning of a French leader who commanded, so to speak, the land armies yet who would control no aviation, even French aviation? This, however, is what seems to have been decided! I fear that in this matter, great haste is being made to execute programs that are entirely unacceptable, and that France, the day she reappears with a regime that represents her, will not acknowledge.

Moreover, "national defense is first of all a state of mind in the nation, and in the government. It is, simply, the determination to defend oneself if attacked" (May 22, 1949). "That is why I am appalled to observe the impotence of the regime under which we languish, which is incapable of organizing, inspiring, directing a national defense worthy of the name" (March 29, 1949). We know this so-called impassive man well enough to imagine his distress at seeing France, despite his warnings, continuing to spoil her chances, one after the other. This distress was to be prolonged for nine years more. And his rage was close to what he had suffered in the prewar years, "when France played the role of a victim waiting her turn. Myself I observed these events without surprise, but not without distress" (*War Memoirs*, I, p. 18). The distress had already begun. And by June 1940, the rage:

Then, at the spectacle of this bewildered people and this military collapse, confronting the enemy's scornful insolence, I was filled with a boundless rage. It was too stupid to be endured! The war was beginning so badly. It must be continued. There was room in the world to do so. . . . What I have been able to do since then, I resolved to do on that day (I, p. 30).

The reservations De Gaulle had formulated as to the Atlantic Pact recurred each time a new initiative from Washington and from London denied an independent France the rank that was hers.

Of the Marshall Plan, which he had always approved in theory, De Gaulle said on November 14, 1949:

The principle of the Marshall Plan is a respectable one, and one for which we must be grateful to the American people. I shall not fail in this obligation. But the way in which it is applied is another matter. If the Marshall Plan is applied to bring pressure upon the foreign policy of the present French regime, then the application is not a good one. There are several reasons to believe that this occasionally happens.

And in regard to the "coal-steel pool," on June 25, 1950:

It is enough to mention such a policy to be certain that the present regime cannot execute it. Worse, if it attempts to do so, there is every reason to fear that France will be deceived. If whatever the intentions of its promoters may be, the so-called "coal-steel pool" provokes doubts among us, it is because the redoubtable obstacles it faces are contrasted, alas! with the inconsistency of our government. I am even told that, for the moment, that government has entirely vanished!

The Rassemblement had diminished, its efforts were scattered, De Gaulle was provisionally to withdraw from his battle, the better to re-initiate it later on. But in the last national session of the RPF, reminding his hearers of the warnings of the past, heralding those still to come, he exclaimed:

Everything has been relinquished before anything was constructed. "Accept," our government has been told, "accept the fact that Germany is once again becoming a Reich." Answer: "We accept the fact!" This was the London agreement. "Abandon your rightful share of the Ruhr coal mines." "We abandon our share!" "Renounce the interallied government of Germany." "We renounce it!" "Agree to no longer having any authority in your zone of occupation." "We agree!" "Recognize that henceforth Germany has equal rights." "Yes, we recognize those rights by so-called contractual agreements!" "Enter the European organizations that are to be established, the coal-steel pool, the defense community, without French Africa!" Answer: "Although this destroys the equilibrium in favor of Germany and comes down to separating the fate of metropolitan France from that of her overseas territories, we will enter the European organizations without these territories!" Last and most recent of these urgent summonses: "Germany must organize her army again. It will be combined with your own in a stateless organization, which will be under American command and which, by the force of events, cannot fail to become the military instrument of German policy. Give us your army!" To which is answered: "Here, to be dissolved in this monstrous organism, is what has been the French Army for a thousand years. Here, in fact, is a project of our own devising for a *European Army,* into which our own will disappear, body and soul!"

After the failure of the Rassemblement, and despite his determination to keep silence, De Gaulle did not hesitate to emerge from his retirement when national defense was at stake. This was his battle against the European Defense Community. During his press conference of February 25, 1953, he cried:

If, during the last conflict, the French Government of the war and the Liberation had submitted to such a regime; if, in the coalition to which it belonged, it had not kept the right and the means of commanding the French troops and had not used them to effect what was indispensable, Koenig would not have been at Bir-Hakeim; Juin would not have played the role he did in Italy; Leclerc would not have taken the Fezzan and would not have been sent, when it was imperative, to Paris; De Lattre would not have defended Alsace, or crossed the Rhine and the Danube; Larminat would not have reduced the Atlantic pockets; Doyen would not have answered for La Brigue and Tenda; the expeditionary force would never have left for Indochina. And I have cited only military episodes, without mentioning the many and enormous political difficulties that supervened between our allies and ourselves, which we have surmounted only because our own means, however reduced they were at the time, continued to belong to us. Obviously, if it had been otherwise, the government established in France upon the Liberation would have been neither more nor less than an Allied Military Government of Occupied Territory—in other words, a foreign government! Pleven, Queuille, Jacquinot, Bidault, Mayer, Auriol, you who were present in the government and who were my ministers, I cannot believe you have forgotten these things!

If he himself was no longer in the government, he influenced, by his mere existence, those who were. "Despite the humiliations of the present, I do not renounce, any more than I did in the past, the greatness of France!" (August 26, 1954.) The National Assembly rejected the plan for a European army.

One of the general's first concerns, when he returned to power, was to demonstrate France's independence in regard to her allies. There was the memorandum of September 24, 1958, whose object was the co-ordination, on a basis of equality, of the relations between Paris, Washington, and London; there were the measures De Gaulle took to show (but this time not by reprimands) that he was not in agreement with the Atlantic Pact as it had been instituted: the French fleet in the Mediterranean would no longer be available to the allied command in case of war; stocks of nuclear warheads and launching platforms for rockets were removed from the national territory; certain pursuit squadrons were recovered by the French command, etc. De Gaulle continued, as in the past, to approve the Atlantic Pact in principle, but he contested its methods of application, and took action accordingly. Let us quote from among many statements the press conference of March 25, 1959:

I note that the two other great world powers of the Atlantic Pact, the United States and Great Britain, have arranged matters so that the greater part of their naval forces are not integrated in NATO. I may add that the Americans and the British have kept in their hands the chief element of their strength, the atomic bombers. The fact that France has reassumed possession of her fleet would certainly not keep her from engaging it, should the need arise, in the common battle in the Mediterranean. Hence there is nothing in this episode that can weaken the Alliance. Quite the contrary. I believe, as a matter of fact, that the Alliance will be all the more vital and stronger when the great States unite in the kind of co-operation in which each bears its own responsibility, rather than in an integration in which peoples and governments are virtually stripped of their role and their responsibility in the realm of their own defense.

Thus a single word, *co-operation,* sufficed to summarize the general's whole policy: a policy directed, as we shall soon discover, as much to the underdeveloped nations as to the most powerful. For De Gaulle there are not two weights, two measures; each State must, without sacrificing any of its independence, collaborate with the rest, not only for the common defense in case of aggression, but for the advancement of the less favored.

Returning, in the course of his press conference of July 29, 1963, to "the elementary necessity of the Atlantic Alliance," celebrating once again the two-hundred-year-old friendship of France and the United States maintained by the fact that "of all the world powers, France is the only one—aside from Russia, I must add—with which the United States has never exchanged cannon fire, and, without exception, the only one that has fought at America's side under conditions never to be forgotten in three wars: the War of Independence, the First and Second World Wars," De Gaulle concluded:

If then, once again, there are divergences between Washington and Paris concerning the organization of the Alliance, the Alliance itself—that is, the fact that in case of a general war, France, with the means she has, will be at the side of the United States, this state of affairs being, I believe, reciprocal—is beyond question, save in the lucubrations of those who make a profession of alarming the timorous by depicting each scratch as an incurable wound. Therefore, neither Franco-American friendship nor the Alliance can be in question; indeed they are not. But it is true that, in dealing with the problems now confronting the two nations, their policies are not always in agreement. There is however nothing fundamentally important or basically distressing, or even surprising in this fact. But we must adapt ourselves, on either side, to this new situation.

So much for the defense of Europe as it was. But now, on November 14, 1949, for Europe as it is to be:

I have always said, I have always believed, that we must create Europe, that we must create her gradually in her economy, in her culture, later in her defense, and even, eventually, in her policy. I have always believed, too, that for Europe to create her unity under satisfactory conditions, she must do so herself, free of all external pressure. I have always said, and I have always believed, that the basis of such a Europe was a direct agreement, without intermediaries, between the French people and the German people, supposing naturally that this agreement was possible. This is not the path that has been followed . . .

The present policy is not a good one. I say as much to our friends in Washington, and I say it to our friends in London. It risks bringing about the collapse of our European organization, and it risks destroying that hope of peace that is, precisely, to create Europe. As for the practice that consists in profiting by the inconsistency of the French Government in order to wrest concessions from it, I am not convinced that it ultimately leads to much gain for its followers . . .

I repeat that the road taken with regard to Germany does not seem to me to be the right one. But I agree that the silence of France counts for a great deal in the matter. There is not, as a matter of fact, a French regime that is France, that says yes or says no, that enlightens the French nation, that leads the others onward, that deals directly with Germany, that seeks to discover whether or not it is possible to create Europe with her. For this, France must be on her feet. That is why we must help her up!

These words spoken fifteen years ago suggest what this supposed adversary of Europe was then alone in realizing:

today Europe is in the process of being created before our eyes, as economy, geography, and history dictate, and as a result of a reconciliation with Germany that existed in De Gaulle's mind at that very moment.

Are his adversaries right in saying that this Franco-German policy ultimately failed? I am writing this the day the Moselle canal is being inaugurated by the President of the French Republic, Charles de Gaulle, with the President of the Federal Republic of Germany and the Grand Duchess of Luxembourg. We see fulfilled in 1964 what De Gaulle had conceived and what he had proclaimed in 1950, when France had scarcely begun her recovery and when she still counted for nothing in the eyes of the English and the Americans. But in regard to this essential problem, I should like once again to return to the source and judge according to the texts. What is involved is not only France, Germany, the end of a bloody history. It is the future of Europe and of the planet that is at stake.

On March 16, 1950, De Gaulle declared apropos of the recent French agreements concerning the Saar:

But this said, and this done, the enormous problem of the relations between the German people and the French people remains. Personally, I am convinced that upon these relations depends the entire fate of Europe and, to a large degree, of the world.

He added:

Chancellor Adenauer, on his side, champions an agreement and perhaps eventually a union between the two peoples. For thirty years, I can tell you, I have followed with interest and consideration the actions and proposals of Konrad Adenauer. On several occasions, I seem to have glimpsed, in this good German's words, a kind of echo to the appeal of Europe, a ruined, broken, bleeding Europe who calls to her children to unite.

On June 25, 1950, closing the national session of the RPF, De Gaulle exclaimed:

Yes, we must hasten to establish the State, Yes, we are determined to recreate national unity. Events urge us on. . . .

For now, despite a thousand obstacles, a lacerated Europe is becoming aware of herself. Before the abyss gaping once again, her children glimpse that the unity of the continent—at least, of that part of it that is free—can and must emerge from the realm of dreams to become a political reality. This reality is ours! We already professed it, even as we were fighting in the thick of the world war, and it is not our fault if the masters of Russia have preferred the reality of domination to it. Of course we have never allowed it to involve the abandonment of what is due to France. That is why we have shown ourselves firm vis-à-vis any and every power when in the past, out of the still-molten matter, the faits accomplis of the future were being forged. But for our part we have done everything so that, despite so much suffering, rancor, and rage, the policy of European unity might be accepted by men's minds.

Further, the unity of Europe requires that the German people and the French people conclude a practical agreement of common action. Their disputes and their battles have, for centuries, led to dislocation. Divided again they would doom our continent to servitude. Together, they would be capable of forming first the economic and cultural basis and later the political basis on which the peoples of our old Europe could ultimately build unity.

Ten years later, and De Gaulle once again at the helm, this policy was translated into reality. Addressing President Luebke, on June 10, 1961, at the end of a dinner given in his honor, the general said:

Thus, Europe begins to fulfill itself, by the mere fact that Germany and France meet. How could I fail to evoke before you, Monsieur le Président, your eminent compatriots who dedicated themselves to that Europe, and first among them that great man Chancellor Konrad Adenauer? There is, here, an international task likely to determine the fate of the universe.

Offering a toast to the President of the Federal Republic, De Gaulle raised his glass "in honor of a Germany henceforth linked to France to effect the union of Europe and thereby to serve humanity." And he said:

God, before Whom so many men, lying underground, died in our great battles, knows how terribly you and we have fought. But in the understanding that now brings the French and the Germans together, what counts above all is the fact that all the wars they have waged no longer correspond to the goals both have now decided to achieve. Not that either of the two peoples wants to forget the courage shown and the sacrifices accepted, when they were shown and accepted without damage to the honor of the combatants. For, if a wicked policy has led to crime and oppression, the reciprocal esteem that the brave feel for each other belongs to the moral patrimony of the human race. But now, by virtue of a kind of miracle born of their past ordeals, their present alarms, and their new forces, everything leads France and Germany to understand and to unite with one another.

Everything, which means the danger that may come from the East, but also two other realities that similarly engage "the life and death of our race":

Once this dike [against totalitarian ambition] is established, will the interior development, begun on both sides under the influence of the same elements, which function in each and which constitute the desire for a better material life as a result of the progress of technology and man's aspiration to a moral condition in accord with his immortal desires—will this evolution bring them together for the salvation and the progress of civilization? Lastly, with peace thus ensured, will we see the well-provided peoples strike down the iron curtains and unite their efforts to abolish hunger, poverty, and ignorance among their underdeveloped comrades?

For several years already, De Gaulle had taken every occasion to indicate the only policy that now seemed to him worthy not only of this or that country, and hence of his own (once independence and security were secured), but of humanity: the abolition of hunger and ignorance through the co-operation of the more favored States, the construction of the just and unified world of tomorrow.

In Rheims, on July 8, 1962, at the end of Chancellor Adenauer's visit, De Gaulle offered this toast:

But the essential element, the fruitful possibility, the divine share of this enormous undertaking is the sentiment of the two peoples. Everything happens, everything is decided in their instinct, their heart, and their mind. . . .

To animate the great European and world-wide enterprise, which the Germans and the Gauls must undertake in common, it was necessary that the soul of the people show its approval on this side of the Rhine. . . . This has occurred in a signal manner. As Germany and France unite to serve freedom, prosperity, fraternity, initially in their own countries, then among the western States of our continent and within the free world on both sides of the Atlantic, and some day perhaps throughout all Europe and thereby for the benefit of all mankind, we can indeed say, such a goal being the very one assigned to our species by the supreme Law of its life, that during your journey through Paris and our provinces, "the voice of the people was the voice of God."

As for Europe, it was essential that she "emerge from the spellbound kingdom of speculation in order to act within the realm of harsh realities." The Brussels Committee was important of course, but the power of decision continued to belong to the governments. "Thus we see, once again, the tendentious impropriety of conception and language by which a certain impulse calls a gathering of international experts, however qualified, *executive*." France being what she is, it was indispensable that the Community include agriculture, "without which, as we have observed, we would have resumed independent action in every regard, and there would have been no Common Market." Lastly, and above all, "the European Community cannot subsist, *a fortiori* develop, without political co-operation":

For this reason and for others, France has proposed co-operation to her five partners. We know that Chancellor Adenauer's government, for its part, approved the proposal and even, as an example, took the initiative for a Franco-German treaty. We know that the draft of political union for the six nations has not yet been concluded, and we know why: those opposed have formulated three conditions that, in our eyes, cannot be met, because they are contradictory and tend either deliberately to place Europe under American hegemony or else to maintain her as a brilliant object of political oratory without her ever becoming a reality.

"No European union," they say, "except by integration into an supranational executive! No European union if England is not a member! No European union, except upon its incorporation into an Atlantic community!" Yet, it is clear that none of the European peoples will consent to trust their fate to an areopagus chiefly composed of foreigners. In any case, this is true of France. It is also clear that England, a great nation and a great State, would be less likely to accept this than anyone else. Lastly, it is clear that to dissolve European policy into a multilateral Atlantic policy would be to deprive Europe of any policy whatsoever and hence one fails to see why she should confederate in the first place (Press conference of January 31, 1964).

To create Europe, but which Europe? That was the question, as De Gaulle was to remark during his next press conference, on July 23, 1964. "Europe must create herself in order to be European. A European Europe signifies that she exists by and for herself, in other words, that in the middle of the world, she has her own policy":

Now this is just what is consciously or unconsciously rejected by some who nonetheless claim they want to see such a Europe created. Basically, the fact that Europe, having no policy, would remain subject to the policy assigned to it from the other side of the Atlantic seems to them, even today, natural and satisfactory.

Hence we have seen a number of otherwise strong and sincere minds advocate for Europe not an independent policy, which indeed they do not conceive of, but an organization incapable of one, dependent in this domain, as in that of defense and economy, upon an Atlantic, that is to say, an American system, and consequently subordinated to what the United States calls its leadership. This organization, baptized "federal," would have as its basis on the one hand, an areopagus of powers from the member States which would be called "executive"; on the other, a Parliament without national qualifications which would be called "legislative." Doubtless each of these two elements would have furnished what would be appropriate; that is, studies in the case of the areopagus and debates in the case of the Parliament. But, certainly, neither of the two would have done what was in fact not wanted; that is to say, neither would have produced a policy . . . Policy is an action, that is to say, a series of decisions made, things done, risks run, all with the support of a people. Only the governments of nations can do this and be answerable for it. It is certainly not impossible to imagine that someday all the peoples of our continent will be united and that there can then be a government of Europe, but it would be absurd to proceed as if that day had come.

De Gaulle, if he thus evoked a united Europe of the future, reminded his listeners that, for the present, France more modestly but more wisely took the initiative of proposing to her five partners in the Rome Treaty "an initial co-operative organization" that would permit them to "begin to live communally, until custom and development gradually draw the links closer." A projected meeting of the six States in Paris, then in Rome, held out hope, but the ill will of Italy and of Benelux left everything up in the air. Great Britain, moreover, had shown in the course of the Brussels negotiations that she was not in a position to accept the common economic rules. Her defense could not be really European, unless it were autonomous in relation to the United States. It appeared, under these conditions, "to the government of the Federal Republic of Germany and to the government of the French Republic that their bilateral co-operation might have some value." Thus was concluded, on the proposal of the German Government, the treaty of January 22, 1963, which the President of the French Republic signed with Chancellor Adenauer.

The consequences of this policy seemed disappointing. Some progress that appeared promising was, of course, made, such as "the happy conclusion of the negotiations on the subject of the Common Market," and on a specific point, the canalization of the Moselle, thanks to which certain regions "each long enclosed in its own system and difficult of access to one another, readily exchange their production, until the period when they can proceed to unify it." In Trèves, on May 26, 1964, De Gaulle declared:

It is this reality that in their time inspired the government leaders who succeeded in settling the question—Robert Schuman and then Mendès-France in Paris, Adenauer in Bonn, and Bech in Luxembourg. We were subsequently to see that nothing could correspond better to the spirit and practice of the European Community, within which six States are now organizing their various economies into a single one. But, however effective the means modern technology affords to enterprises such as those whose happy conclusion we are celebrating today may be; however rational an undertaking that will multiply the relations and exchanges among the regions along the Moselle and the Rhine; however powerful the developments that at present impel Germany, Italy, Holland, Belgium, Luxembourg, and France to unite their economic activities into a whole, the mutual control of this river by three States could not have been achieved without the impetus of a policy. Yes, certainly, of a policy, and how vast and new a policy. . . .

Doubtless history will regard as one of the chief facts of human life the extraordinary change that, in the course of the last two decades, has led the German people and the French people, first to abandon their old hostility, then to join, side by side, in various international organizations designed either for security purposes, such as the Atlantic Alliance, or for economic progress, such as the European Common Market, and finally to practice together a regular and specific co-operation with a view to common action in all domains.

Two months later, during his July 23 press conference, De Gaulle changed his tone. Instead of emphasizing the progress made, he declared that if the Franco-German treaty had indeed produced "minor results," and if it had led the two governments and their administrations to practice contacts that he personally considered useful and that were in any case extremely pleasant, it could not be said that a line of common action had thus far resulted:

Assuredly, there is not and cannot be, strictly speaking, an opposition between Bonn and Paris. But whether the issue is the effective solidarity of France and Germany as to their defense; or the new organization to be effected within the Atlantic Alliance; or the attitude and action to be taken vis-à-vis the East, particularly in regard to Moscow's satellites, or, correlatively, the frontiers and nationalities in central and eastern Europe, or the recognition of China and the diplomatic and economic action Europe could take toward this great people; or peace in Asia, notably in Indochina and Indonesia; or the aid to be given to the developing nations in Africa, Asia, and Latin America; or the establishment of the Agricultural Common Market and consequently the future of the Community of the Six Nations—in none of these issues can it be said that Germany and France have yet reached an agreement to effect a policy together, and no one can deny that this is because Bonn has not believed, up until now, that such a policy must be European and independent. If this state of affairs persists, it risks ultimately generating doubt in the French people, anxiety in the German people, and in their four partners of the Rome Treaty a reinforced propensity to remain where they are until, perhaps, their ultimate dispersal.

The press conferences of the President of the Republic—the host of journalists from all over the world, the splendid setting; the swaying curtain, the tall man who appears, majestic, simple, and who speaks not only to those present, but to millions of living men, and not only to millions of living men, but to the generations not yet born who will also see and hear De Gaulle—for history, henceforth, will be illustrated by those who have made it, whatever we may say about it—these new techniques will end up by pushing aside the old political parties and even the parliaments. Soon the old chessboard will no longer be of any use at all.

I stand aside from politics for a moment and consider De Gaulle from the viewpoint of the television spectator. I tell myself that the success of the "act," its perfection, could reach such a pitch only as a result of the truth of the character—of the televised character which itself is true only because it is the reflection of an authentic man. De Gaulle may have advanced under a mask at certain moments of his life. But on this July 23, 1964, he holds his mask in his hand and speaks to the world without for an instant seeking to deceive it. With Germany, for the moment at least, the situation seems to have reached a standstill. And De Gaulle says as much. We must wait. What he does not say is that everything depends on what will happen tomorrow between Johnson and the Kremlin, and on what they say to each other by telephone. The Common Market, which we believed to be pregnant with Europe, may have a miscarriage, and may die of it. The best gambler can play only with the cards he has in his hand: in De Gaulle's, neither kings nor aces are abundant.

This is the way De Gaulle speaks about Europe. I do not believe that anything inspires more contempt in him than the need, that fixed idea in certain French minds, to dissolve a France grown weak and small into a great whole where she would become, in a sense, invisible. In the renunciation based on the false shame advocated by certain of our "Europeans" there is one calculation: since France is no longer the great nation, no longer anything more than an old province of the new Europe, they count on its being a privileged province in so far as it is the dependent of the United States of America.

For what chiefly counts in their eyes is this allegiance

with the great people of the West. As they see it, De Gaulle's inexpiable fault is to have denounced that allegiance.

But on this point is not De Gaulle himself caught in a contradiction? It has taken him no more than a few years, really only a few months, to assure the French nation a place in the first rank despite its reduced means. But he questions no more than his Anglo-American and Russian allies the necessity of possessing the material means of greatness, if he seeks to be great. No more than they does he believe in a purely spiritual power: that is the role of the Church. A free people cannot depend on any other for its defense . . . I have not entered into the atomic controversy, and I shall not enter into it to conclude my essay, for I am divided on this subject; a whole part of myself rebels against this absurd complicity with powers capable of destroying the planet. But how could I dismiss De Gaulle's reasons?

In truth, the atomic weapon remains the visible sign of an exigency, an ambition, a claim—legitimate or unjustified? That is the entire debate. And since even those who condemn it today do not believe that, once they are its masters, they can renounce it henceforth, I am inclined to believe that what De Gaulle has attempted in every realm to restore France to her true place is irreversible.

I have had occasion to speak and to write to calm the minds of those Frenchmen who hardly dare breathe once we take two steps without the permission of the United States: "What are you afraid of? It's always the most powerful who has his hands tied. It won't take you eight days, after De Gaulle, to put the country back where De Gaulle picked it up, under the boots of the Anglo-American powers . . ." I have written this and said it. But to tell the truth, I no longer believe it: De Gaulle's successor, even if he is the most determined adversary of atomic armament, will find himself committed to such a program despite himself, and determined in his course despite himself, and everything will follow in the direction of independence.

Will De Gaulle have time to change our nature by changing our habits (our institutions)? In truth, it was our nature as a great sovereign nation that was transformed under the last two Republics, and to a large degree because of the German threat, into the role of a petitioner who was free to indulge in the stupidest maneuvers at home, which led straight to death, on condition that it consented, in foreign policy, to be a docile pawn on the American chessboard in the game that the Pentagon certainly does not always win.

One does not have to have De Gaulle's brain to realize this. But one would have to be De Gaulle to believe, or to act as if he believed, that a little France, confronting the United States, possesses the possibility of independence and of refusal.

Relying upon whom? Certainly not on her allies in the Common Market, who envy France (when they no longer scorn her) and sound the alarm themselves once the guardian shadow of Albion or of American capitalism no longer protects them. As for the world outside the blocs, the most dispersed and disarmed world of all, France may take the measure of what can be expected from that world in the United Nations . . . If I were to speak my inmost thought, I would say that De Gaulle's France sometimes reminds me of M. Seguin's goat, the valiant little goat that struggled all night long, only to be devoured at dawn by the wolf.

It is in my hours of doubt that this thought comes to me. And then I wonder: once again, what do we risk? There is no wolf in history, even if events were to go against us. And there will not be one so long as it is to the Russians' advantage to maintain peace in the world. Even if it were conquered, M. Seguin's goat would get back to its stable and its pasture in the shadow of the Stars and Stripes.

But the little goat can win; and the entire subject of this book is that its victory has already been demonstrated by Charles de Gaulle, when France was at the nadir of her history.

Did De Gaulle, too, not have his hours of doubt, knowing the French as he does? I have not corrected one contradiction that recurs throughout this book because it is a contradiction that exists in myself as well. I have related De Gaulle to the family of minds that believe that nations are perishable and that France will perish if she does not renounce the mores that, under the last two republics, have nearly caused her ruin. This is the family of Maurras. And yet De Gaulle also belongs to the family of Péguy. Even in the depths of the abyss, this Frenchman feels unbeaten, immortal, eternal. It is a contradiction that explains the oscillation of Gaullist thought: the alarm he has sought to keep awake in us in the face of the disaster; and, once the disaster has fallen, the hope based on the facts and on an analysis that history has verified.

Such a hope also derives from a mystique: "France, because she is France . . ." This sublime stupidity is one we hear often. What does De Gaulle really think of it? When he lets his mind wander, how far does he let it go? Let us not forget, De Gaulle continually envisions the possibility of total destruction. He faces that risk, directly. He assumes it, as he has always assumed whatever is inescapable.

Even if there were no such risk, even if the atomic weapon did not exist, the fact would remain that when men possessed only an insignificant power of destruction empires followed one another and collapsed, were covered by sand or devoured by the jungle.

With what promise of eternity do we flatter ourselves when our chances of being annihilated are so much greater than those that operated, in the course of history, against civilizations of which only a few indecipherable traces remain?

We do not know, we shall never know, if De Gaulle some-times lets his mind brood over this abyss. There is nothing of Chateaubriand about him but the style, certainly not the notion that there will be nothing valid left in the world once he himself has disappeared from it. A world without Chateaubriand no longer interested Chateaubriand. What counts in De Gaulle's eyes, in De Gaulle, is the France he has had the madness to believe he embodied; and this mad-ness was not a madness, but the most intense reality. So long as he has a thought left, then, it will be for France, and devoted to making France last, and therefore to keeping her from reverting to her bad political customs.

No, De Gaulle is not a man to say "après moi, le déluge!" But a man to "bring it about so that . . ."—that is an ex-pression familiar to him; to bring it about so that there can no longer be a deluge after him, at least not because of the failure of institutions, which still depends in large part on him, so long as he still belongs to the world of the living.

What he is not responsible for is the choice of the man who doubtless already exists and who will succeed him. For it is absurd to imagine a world after De Gaulle in which we could do without a De Gaulle—that is, without a thinking mind and a sovereign will. The situation that has made De Gaulle necessary will survive him, and that, to my mind, will deprive his adversaries of their revenge. He will no longer be here; but what makes *them* undesirable, in the absolute sense of the word, will always be here. Gaullism without De Gaulle will in a sense be imposed by a rea soned instinct of self-preservation. What has been saved, contrary to all expectations, since 1940, we will not gamble with again, we will not risk further, even to satisfy a certain idea of democracy, which a certain race of Frenchmen has great difficulty getting out of its head.

The future belongs to no one. But what De Gaulle has created, what he has made forever, that absolute history which is also his own history—how does he judge it from the vantage point, the promontory he has now reached? As a victory? Does he feel he has won the game?

In truth, all human politics are a failure. No great political concept is ever carried out as it was conceived. From this viewpoint, De Gaulle, in his black hours, may decide that he has not achieved his goal. At least it occurs to him, I imagine, to ponder those points where the outcome has not corresponded to his expectation, where he himself has been disappointed and hence disappointing to others: Africa, what he had received from it and what he had hoped for—the French Union that was his only chance of confronting the two atomic empires with an empire of a hundred million human beings; fate has robbed him of this. And De Gaulle himself is the only witness of his greatness, which is to have turned that frustration into an advantage, for his enemies will forever force him to assume responsibility for the liquidation of the Empire, and especially for the loss of Algeria.

Let us turn then, one last time, to the texts. Let us ask De Gaulle himself to become, in this great trial, the judge of De Gaulle. It is after hearing him that we can give him the answer that will be history's. De Gaulle has never been so great as when history has set its traps for him and, specifically, the trap of decolonization.

IN EVOKING once again, on July 8, 1962, the "depths of the French soul," De Gaulle, addressing Germany through the man who then embodied her, evoked "a great European and world-wide enterprise," an enterprise ultimately "to the benefit of all mankind." What henceforth appears as one of his most constant preoccupations is one of his oldest projects. As early as January 30, 1944, he declared, at the opening of the Brazzaville conference:

At the moment the present world war began, the necessity of establishing on new bases the conditions for the development of our Africa, for the human progress of its inhabitants, and for the exercise of French sovereignty were already apparent.

As always, the war itself precipitated the evolution of that necessity. First of all, because it has been, until now, largely an African war and therefore, both the absolute and relative importance of Africa's resources, communications, and forces has appeared in the harsh light of the theaters of military operations. But subsequently and especially because this war has as its stake neither more nor less than the condition of man, and because, under the pressure of the psychic forces which it has everywhere released, each individual raises his head, looks beyond the present, and questions his fate.

If there is any imperial power that should be inspired by the lesson of what has happened to choose nobly and liberally the road to the new age in which it will seek to lead the sixty million who are associated with the fate of its own forty-two million, that power is France! . . .

We believe in particular that from the point of view of the development of resources and communications, the African continent must in large measure constitute a whole. But in French Africa, as in all the other territories where men are living under our flag, there is no genuine progress if men on their natal soil do not profit from it morally and materially, if they do not gradually raise themselves to the level where they can participate in the management of their own country's affairs. It is the duty of France to make this ideal a reality.

Such is the goal toward which we must now turn our steps. We shall not conceal from ourselves the distance we must cover in order to reach it.

At the time, such a position was revolutionary. It determined the fate of the future African States, long before their accession to power. Certainly what De Gaulle was thinking of in this spring of 1944, was that only those who were born in each territory should participate in its administration. Contrary to De Gaulle's expectations, the distance to be covered was to become increasingly shorter, once the process was set in motion. Here again the general was capable of adapting his thought and his action to an evolution that he had foreseen but whose rapidity once it had begun he could have predicted no more than anyone else. On August 27, 1946, he could still declare:

On this crucial point, the draft of the Constitution limits itself to asserting the principle of "self-determination," which, in the present state of development of the overseas territories and given the co-operation of the other great powers, could lead the populations only to agitation, dislocation, and finally to foreign domination. Further, the draft specifies nothing that is constructive, and this deficiency is a grave one.

The Constitution should, on the contrary, affirm and impose solidarity with France on all the overseas territories. It should, in particular, place beyond question the pre-eminent responsibility and, consequently, the rights of France in regard to the foreign policy of the entire French Union, the defense of all its territories, common communications, and economic measures that concern the entire system. This granted, it must be recognized that each actual territorial and national entity must be organized in such a way that it can develop according to its own character, whether it already constitutes a State linked to France by treaty, or whether it becomes a territory enjoying an autonomy in proportion to its development, or whether it is incorporated into the French Republic. Lastly, certain institutions of a federal character that are common to metropolitan France and the overseas territories should be created: Presidency of the French Union, Council of the French Union, Ministries assigned to federal activities.

And again, in the speech at Épinal, on September 29, 1946:

It seems to us necessary that the French Union be a union and that it be French; in other words, that the overseas peoples who are linked to our destiny have the capacity to develop according to their own character and to accede to the control of their own affairs in proportion to their progress; that they be associated with France for the discussion of their interests; and that France maintain her pre-eminence in regard to what is common to all: foreign policy, national defense, communications, economic affairs of the entire system. These conditions imply, on the one hand, local institutions appropriate to each of the territories, and on the other, common institutions: Council of States, Assembly of the French Union, Ministries assigned to affairs common to all.

But in the Place de la République, on September 4, 1958, De Gaulle declared:

The relations between metropolitan France and the overseas territories require a profound adaptation. The universe is filled with currents that jeopardize the future of the human race and oblige France to protect herself, while she represents the interests of measure, peace, and fraternity dictated by her vocation.

By this period, and despite the gravity of the Algerian situation, De Gaulle saw further. He recognized in Africa

an element of a vaster problem, the problem of co-operation. In Blois, on May 9, 1959, he exclaimed: "Then France
will be the champion of that co-operation, which is indispensable to humanity":

It is her genius, it is her vocation to assume moral leadership;
in any case to point the way. She will do so in all conscience and
without letting herself be deceived by any propaganda. Without
retreating before any threat, so that, thanks to her, the two bil-
lions of whom I spoke may find a hope and may have aid in
gradually raising themselves to that level where a man achieves
—whether he is white, black, yellow, or brown—dignity, prosperity, and fraternity.

On June 5, 1959, De Gaulle declared in Saint-Flour:

Externally, our country has a human task to accomplish, and it
must give the signal, must take the initiative in the co-operation
that more favored peoples like ourselves must bring to those who
are not, or who are less so, and who comprise the great majority
of the earth's inhabitants. It is in this task that, when the occasion
arises, if it should present itself in a conference, France will, I
repeat, take the initiative. This is the undertaking it will propose
to its three great partners so that, whatever their regime, whatever their doctrine, whatever their disputes, they may decide—
they who have every means of co-operating—to co-operate for the
good of their two billion brothers whose standard of living must
be raised, who must be brought to the level of dignity and
fraternity.

And, on the same day, in Aurillac:

France is on this earth to promote and to serve our fellow men.
. . . This is France's human vocation . . . upon the whole of this
earth. There are, upon the planet, about two billion eight hundred million inhabitants. Two billion of them are far from having
achieved a level of development analogous to our own. And there
are eight hundred million who, despite the difficulties we sometimes experience by reason of politics, doctrines, and regimes,
have, to various degrees, advanced beyond the others. The great
problem of the world and of the age is to bring these eight hun-

dred million to unite in a co-operation above and beyond their rivalries, for the development of the two billion others. And it must be France that sets the example in this matter, that takes the initiative with her three great partners in the world—a task she is disposed to undertake and will undertake, as soon as she finds the opportunity to do so.

These lines date from 1959. Thus in 1964 De Gaulle is not seeking some dark revenge, at least in regard to essentials; he is not resorting to aggression toward the United States— no, he is pursuing the only policy that concerns him today, because it concerns the world in its honor, its happiness, and because our nation can play a decisive role in this development of humanity. It is remarkable that De Gaulle should feel that in comparison to this grand design the rivalries between doctrines and regimes and "the difficulties" that result from them lose their importance; that further he should call upon the Soviet Union to collaborate with the other powers involved in the common undertaking. In 1959, however, the Algerian affair was not settled. De Gaulle could not yet devote himself to what would become, a few years later, his basic preoccupation.

In the course of a parliamentary conference on March 23, 1964, in Fort-de-France, De Gaulle, according to witnesses, declared: "Policy is reality or nothing. I take Martinique as it is, and I observe that sentiments, taste, instinct—everything here is French." Similarly he was obliged to take Algeria as it was, and to observe that it was not French. His policy was imposed upon him by the realities which so many passions, and often legitimate ones, concealed from those born there, who could rightfully consider the country their own. And here too De Gaulle has clung closely to what was the reality of the moment, gradually adapting himself to its demands, until the day he knew that France would have to consent to leave this land where she had done so much, and where so many of her children for several generations had been born, worked, loved, suffered, died. It is easy to set De Gaulle in contradiction with himself. Beyond the famous "I have understood you" of June 4, 1958, he had been able to declare, eleven years before, on August 18, 1947:

Sovereignty of France! This means, first of all, that we must not permit the fact that Algeria is part of our domain to be questioned in any way, either at home or abroad. This also means that there is no matter involving Algeria that the French Government —its executive, legislative, judiciary systems—can alienate its right and its duty to decide in the last resort. This means, finally, that the authority of the French Republic must be exercised thoroughly and powerfully on the spot, and that the Governor General, invested by the State, can answer only to the French Government.

After which, visiting Algiers as the leader of the RPF the following October 12, he chose to say "to those Frenchmen, Moslems or not, who are deluded by the dream of secession: You are deceiving yourselves and others! Your future as proud and free men, and the future of your children, is to be found only with France and in France." He added on the subject of this Algeria, "an integral part of France":

The good of Algeria consists in this: that France pursue and develop here the admirable enterprise she began a hundred and seventeen years ago. This undertaking has been accomplished, under her authority, by the effort of her sons from the metropolitan country and by the labor of the others. It is these three elements that have made Algeria what she is. If France ever permitted one of the three to be displaced, there is no doubt whatever that the entire structure would crumble and that Algeria would immediately be plunged into a confusion from which no one would benefit except the abettors of universal discord.

The authority of France must therefore be asserted as clearly and as powerfully here as on any other French soil. The Algerians of metropolitan origin must confidently continue all that they have undertaken, without fear of ever being submerged. The

French Moslems of Algeria must find, in the esteem of our people, in the context of French sovereignty, and in their own personal status, all possibilities of improving their destiny as their country advances and of exercising their capacities as they develop them. What I myself proclaimed in Constantine on December 12, 1943, and promulgated by decree on March 7, 1944, corresponds to these principles. Any policy whose effect, on the fallacious pretext of a reverse evolution, is to reduce the rights and the duties of France in this country, or to discourage the inhabitants of metropolitan origin, who were and remain the yeast of Algeria, or lastly, to lead the French Moslems to believe that they are warranted in separating their fate from that of France, any such policy would merely, in truth, open the door to decadence.

Reality at that time was the reality of a French Algeria. But that reality changed. Then too, there was that other reality, at the time, of a danger of world war which, according to Paul-Marie de la Gorce, whose analysis deserves to be repeated here, explains to a large degree De Gaulle's position on that day in Algiers, though on the preceding May 15, he had insisted in Bordeaux on the desirable autonomy of the territories of the French Union: "convinced that nothing would stand in the way of a Soviet offensive on the European continent, De Gaulle regarded a new exile of the French Government as likely; in this case, it was essential to avoid the servitudes of a refuge in a foreign country—from which he had suffered so greatly in London. Tunisia and Morocco would not fail to reinforce their separationist status. Dakar was too far; Algeria alone afforded French sovereignty the shelter of French soil." All the possibilities, all the probabilities, fortunately, did not occur: if the general's realism was, on this point, not borne out by the facts, it was confirmed by many others. Notably when he was obliged to convince himself and, gradually, the French that Algeria had the right to self-determination. And that our nation would emerge stronger from this amputation, and greater—that it would gain in influence what it lost in power.

Hence, in the speech in Constantine on October 3, 1958, in which he launched the Five Year Plan his government had just established for Algeria, De Gaulle, if he gave details as to "the enormous political, economic, social, and cultural enterprise" that only France could fulfill, hedged as to the future and reserved the margin for his action that the development of the situation might (and did) render necessary, saying: "To what will this profound development lead? In regard to the political status of Algeria, I believe it is quite useless to put into words what the enterprise will in any case gradually bring into being." Similarly, on the following October 23, in the general's first press conference after his return to power, he declared:

Some say: "But what political conditions will the government permit one to debate?" I answer: Algerian politics belong to Algeria herself. The fact that shots are fired does not give us the right to decide. When a democratic course of action lies open, when the citizens are able to express their will, no other course is acceptable. Now this course is open in Algeria. The referendum has taken place. In November there will be legislative elections. In March will come the elections of the municipal councils. In April, the election of the senators.

What will be the result? It is a matter of evolution. In any case, an enormous material and moral transformation is under way in Algeria. France, because it is her duty and because she alone has the power to do so, is effecting this transformation. As the development proceeds, political solutions will take shape.

I believe, as I have already said, that such solutions will have as their basis—this is the nature of things—the courageous personality of Algeria and her close association with metropolitan France. I also believe that the coalition completed by the Sahara, will join with the States of Morocco and Tunisia for the common progress. Sufficient unto each day is the heavy labor thereof. But who will ultimately triumph? You will see that it will be a fraternal civilization.

Nothing has invalidated, in its essentials, what *the nature of things* permitted De Gaulle, in October 1958 (and doubtless long before), to foresee. Let us note the importance he gave at that date, and for Algeria herself, to the opening of the *democratic course* that he is so often accused, and always wrongly, of not taking in France. As the situation developed, political solutions did as a matter of fact take shape. And if the solution that prevailed was not the one De Gaulle might have wished, it has nevertheless up to now consecrated beyond all expectations a collaboration of independent and socialist Algeria with France. What has triumphed, despite so much suffering, so many lacerations, is indeed, until today at least, a *fraternal civilization.*

On September 16, 1959, De Gaulle declared:

Taking into account all the elements—Algerian, national, and international—I consider it necessary that the recourse to self-determination be proclaimed as of today. In the name of France and of the Republic, by virtue of the power invested in me by the Constitution to consult the citizens, provided God grants me life and the people give me a hearing, I pledge myself to asking, on the one hand, the Algerians in their twelve departments to make their definitive choice, and on the other, the French to ratify that choice.

Provided God grants me life and the people give me a hearing . . . The words have a simplicity, almost a Christian humility, about them. During his press conference of April 11, 1961, in which he declared that "France would regard with equanimity a solution by which Algeria would cease to belong to her domain, a solution that, in other times, might have seemed disastrous for us and that we at present regard with a perfectly calm heart," De Gaulle answered the "people who will say: 'But it is the rebellion that leads you to think in that way!'" and added:

Hence it is not the rebellion that makes me speak as I do, though I grant that the events that have occurred, are occurring in Algeria, have confirmed me in what I have thought and indicated for over twenty years, without joy it is true—and you will understand why—but with the certainty of thus serving France well.

And the general reminded his listeners that since Brazzaville he had never ceased asserting that the populations attached to France must become the masters of their own fate; that in 1941 he granted independence to the mandated States of Syria and Lebanon; in 1945 gave the right to vote to all Africans, including the Moslem Algerians; in 1947 approved the status of Algeria, which "if it had been applied would in all likelihood have led to the gradual establishment of an Algerian State associated with France"; gave his consent to the end of the protectorate treaties with Tunisia and Morocco. In 1958, "having resumed the direction of affairs," he and his government created the French Community, then recognized and aided the independence of the new States of black Africa and of Madagascar. "Not having returned in time to forestall the Algerian insurrection, upon taking office I proposed to its leaders that we conclude a 'peace of the brave' and begin political discussions." In 1959 he proclaimed the right of the Algerian populations to self-determination and the desire of France to accept the solution imposed by its choice, whatever it might be, subsequently declaring on many occasions that Algeria would be Algerian, evoking the birth of its future Republic, and renewing offers of negotiation. "It is not our doing that the Melun discussions were broken off. At the same time, I have put down the conspiracies that attempted to force me to sustain the integration. In 1961, I asked the French people to give me a vote of confidence, which was accomplished by a massive referendum, and I again invited the men of the rebellion to make contact with our representatives." And he added:

In short, we are proving every day that an Algeria that belongs to herself is in no way contrary to the policy of France. What, then, is that policy? It is one of decolonization. But if I have undertaken and pursued it for a long time, it is not only because it was possible to foresee and subsequently observe the enormous liberation movement that the world war and its consequences released throughout the world and that, moreover, the rival claims of the Soviet Union and of America did not fail to dramatize.

If I have done so, it is also and above all because it seemed to me contrary to the present interest and new ambition of France to remain subject to obligations and responsibilities that are no longer in accord with what her power and her influence demand. Moreover, this is also true for other nations. . . . I mean that the reasons that, in the past, led certain civilized peoples to take others who were not civilized under their direct control, these reasons are vanishing utterly even in the minds of the former colonial powers. It now appears to the most powerful nations that their future, their salvation, and the possibilities of their global action reside in their own development and in the co-operation of the former colonies, much more than in the dominations imposed on the allogeneous peoples.

And on March 26, 1962, in regard to Algeria, the "young State about to be born," and to France:

For both nations, it is therefore in accord with reason that, transcending the recent strife, they organize their co-operation with the French Republic as some twelve African Republics and the Republic of Madagascar have done, under the conditions appropriate to them. This enterprise of replacing and everywhere transforming what she accomplished by colonization, is, no doubt, one of the greatest and, perhaps, one of the most fruitful undertakings France has attempted since she appeared on the face of the earth.

On January 31, 1964, De Gaulle emphasized the continuity of his policy since the days of Free France:

To recognize the right of self-determination on the part of all peoples who were not strictly our own but who depended upon us, to control matters so that ultimately, and despite the ensuing

strife, this right might be realized in agreement with us, and that
subsequently a splendid and friendly co-operation might be established between us and the new States—this was indeed the
policy of France, as proclaimed twenty years ago in Brazzaville
by Free France and as achieved by the Republic, once it could
finally disengage itself from a regime of impotence and confusion.

"Co-operation is henceforth one of France's great ambitions":

Certainly this costs us dear. . . . There is not a single nation
in the world that devotes such a proportion of what it is doing for
itself to the progress of others. After us, the nation that comes
first from this point of view is America. Certainly the United
States offers many nations a co-operation whose total effect, in
absolute value, is much more considerable. But in relation to her
means, the aid America furnishes is not, in percentage, half of
our own. As for the Soviet Union, the percentage is less still.

It is true that this co-operation is not only a one-way affair.
The maintenance of active commercial relations with the Arab
States and the black African States that have concluded agreements with us, and the development rights granted us in regard
to certain raw materials, notably a share of Algerian petroleum,
are of real value to us. Assuredly what we gain from them is far
below what we are giving. But the mere fact that there is an exchange does not seem to us negligible, and it is quite evident
that we would be reluctant to furnish a great deal to those who
would provide us nothing in return. Yet the importance that co-
operation assumes lies less in the figures and the immediate profits than in the advantages of a general order which it can assure
us and our partners in the future.

What De Gaulle was expressing here about the young
independent States to which our country was granting aid,
he once asserted about Europe and France herself, when
the aid in question was not given, but received:

However, I wish to emphasize that it is Europe's responsibility
to repay her creditors, as much by the reinforcement of their
security as by the development of great international exchanges.

For, in the relations to be established and in the agreements to be concluded between the two sides of the Atlantic, the issue must be one of co-operation and not of dependence, or we will risk compromising everything to the misfortune of all (Compiègne, March 7, 1948).

Another example of the continuity of De Gaulle's thought. And further, a proof of his desire for independence and his insistence on justice. With, already, the word *co-operation* that, as we have suggested, De Gaulle used both to define his policy in the realm of mutual defense and for the support to be given to the underdeveloped States. There are, however, many in France who would prefer to stop giving aid to the new nations. And just as in Brazzaville, on January 30, 1944, De Gaulle raised the question himself the better to answer it ("Wait!—that is doubtless the advice we could expect from the false prudence of the past. The war, it would remind us, is not over, and who can tell what the peace, tomorrow, will be. Moreover, has France not, alas! concerns more immediate than the future of her overseas territories?"), so in his speech of April 16, 1964, De Gaulle answered this opposition merely by formulating their claim: "There is, finally, no lack of critics to declare . . . : let us stop aiding the progress of peoples who, the world over, aspire to our civilization. Thus we can increase our allocations to State employees and to collective investments." De Gaulle went on to say:

As for cutting off the friendly, reciprocal, and calculated co-operation that we are practicing with a certain number of developing States, this move would, first of all, alienate them from us and leave our place open to others. It would also lead to severing ourselves from vast opportunities of economic, technological, and cultural action, instead of making them accessible. Last and most important, such action would be equivalent to denying our rightful role in the evolution that is leading so many peoples of Africa, Asia, and Latin America to develop themselves in their turn without surrendering to either of the two hegemonies, which tend to divide up the universe, since Western Europe will not or cannot organize itself in such a way as to establish equilibrium. Why, then, should France, herself in a period of expansion, stand apart from a movement whose source comes in large measure from her traditional genius and on which the peace and the fate of the world ultimately depend?

De Gaulle attaches such an importance to national independence—the primary condition, in his eyes, of all European or ultimately world-wide organization—that a nation that enforces respect for such independence immediately wins his favor, whatever its regime. When the People's Republic of China gave proof of its independence of the Soviet Union, De Gaulle decided he could accord it diplomatic recognition (which he had believed was desirable for a long time), declaring on January 31, 1964:

It is true that Soviet Russia initially afforded China considerable support. . . . This was the time when the Kremlin utilizing, here as elsewhere, its rigorous preponderance within the Communist bloc to maintain Russia's supremacy over the peoples subject to its dictatorship, counted on keeping China under its control and thereby dominating Asia. But that illusion has been dispelled. Doubtless a certain doctrinal solidarity still remains between the regimes established in Moscow and in Peking, which can manifest itself in the world rivalry of ideologies. But under a cloak growing daily more ragged the inevitable difference in national policies shows. The least that can be said on this subject is that in Asia, where the frontier between the two States, from the Hindu Kush to Vladivostok, is the longest in the world, Russia's interest, which is to conserve and maintain, and China's, which is to grow and aggrandize, cannot be identified. The result is that the attitude and the action of a people of seven hundred million inhabitants are in fact controlled only by its own government.

But beyond all the reasons that have incited France to recognize the Peking government without thereby "implying any approval of the regime that at present prevails in China," chief among which is that "France is doing no more than recognizing the world as it is," there is this reason in particular, formulated during the same press conference:

Above all, it is possible, in the tremendous evolution of the world, that by multiplying the relations among peoples we are serving the cause of mankind, that is, the cause of wisdom, progress, and peace. It is possible that such contacts contribute to the gradual attenuation of the dramatic contrasts and oppositions between the different camps dividing the world. It is possible that in this way the souls of men, wherever they may be on this earth, will meet a little sooner at the rendezvous that France gave the universe some hundred and seventy-five years ago, the rendezvous of liberty, equality, and fraternity.

As De Gaulle also said that day, "the development of the nations of the world, and in particular of those that hitherto have merely begun this great impulse, is the world question par excellence." Upon this enterprise "depends the salvation of the race." Thus he was aware of *serving the cause of mankind,* not only when he recognized, in his country's name, an independent state of seven hundred million inhabitants, but when he offered the new States the aid of yesterday's colonial power. Explaining, on January 31, 1964, "how high are the goals, and how powerful the motives of co-operation," De Gaulle added:

But it is here that the undertaking transcends its African context and in truth constitutes a world policy. By this means, France can make herself felt in other countries, on other continents, countries in the process of development which appeal to us by instinct and by nature, countries seeking assistance that, accorded in the proper spirit, will induce them to associate us directly with their progress and, reciprocally, to participate in all that is France. . . . No doubt, the material effort we French are in a position to furnish in this regard is limited by our resources, which are not enormous. But our own continuing internal progress affords us means that are increasing from year to year. Moreover, for us the problem is often providing our friends with the ferment of technological and cultural progress, which demands human talents and friendly understanding even more than money. Lastly, we may suppose that a Europe eventually organized as we propose would aspire, jointly with us, to a larger part in this enterprise on which the fate of our race depends. Everything connects: what we are attempting in order to build an independent Europe combines with what we are doing for the peoples rising within our civilization. Yes, co-operation is henceforth a great ambition of France.

In his address given on March 16, 1964, at the University of Mexico, De Gaulle declared:

Above and beyond distances which are shrinking, ideologies which are wasting away, policies which are losing ground, and unless humanity one day annihilates itself in a monstrous destruction, the fact that will dominate the future is the unity of our universe. One cause, that of mankind; one necessity, that of world progress, and consequently, that of aid to all nations that seek it for their development; one duty, that of peace—these are, for mankind, the very conditions of its life.

We have already heard De Gaulle take account of the "ideologies which are wasting away," in his speeches of June 5, 1959, in Saint-Flour and in Aurillac. He was looking far into the future, farther than 1964, for even today such remarks seem largely premature, if not simply rash. De Gaulle assuredly visited Mexico to further the cause of French policy. He declared there, for example, on March 17, 1964, that in the solidarity being created between the two nations, it was essential that "the goal, the attitude, the action, in a word, the policies of Mexico and of France not be in opposition and that, in fact, they be brought into agreement." De Gaulle specified: "Here, on the other hand, is Mexico . . . the Mexico that, without in any way belittling the natural and fruitful aspects of her significant relations with her great neighbor to the north, is drawn by all kinds of affinities toward the European nations, and first of all, I daresay, toward my own." But the final objective,

beyond the interests of either country, was of a global order. Calling in the same speech for a cultural and scientific
exchange, De Gaulle could say to the representatives of the
Mexican people: "This is what would make France and
Mexico true and good companions in the enterprise of civilization which today galvanizes the world."

A year earlier almost to the day, at a banquet at the
Élysée in honor of the President of the United States of
Mexico, De Gaulle had said, on March 26, 1963:

But it also happens that your nation's rise has appeared in our
age, when the world is at grips with tremendous problems and
limitless dangers. It happens, at the same time, that the evolution
of Latin America, of which your own ascension affords an example, is today essential to Europe and to France. The fate of humanity will depend in large part on what becomes of this part of
the world in economic, social, cultural, and political terms; on the
results of its gestation today; and particularly on what Mexico
will strive to do and succeed in doing.

Thus he announced his major South American policy
which was to reach its flowering the following year. De
Gaulle had spoken, on that March 26, 1963, in Paris, of co-
operation—as he was to do on March 17, 1964, in Mexico
City. In the course of the luncheon given him that day in
the National Palace by President Adolfo Lopez Mateos, De
Gaulle, before raising his glass in honor of his host, declared:

But when, among two peoples, both heart and reason are in
agreement, a policy is established. It is, then, the policy that was
marked, Monsieur le Président, by the important and moving
visit you made to Paris last year, the policy that was further defined by the subsequent agreement signed by our two governments, and the policy that the magnificent reception you are
giving me today manifests to the entire world. Yes, to the entire
world. For if this policy is Franco-Mexican, it is thereby world-
wide. That individual relations should be established between
your nation, which is the vitals of Latin America, and mine,

which is essential to Europe and also extending its influence and its activity in Africa and in Asia, is a fact whose consequences can fortunately transcend both our States.

Particularly since you and we have no intention, by reason of this new fact, of excluding or even reducing the relations, the currents, the contacts that link us to our respective neighbors and to other peoples; particularly, too, since there is what appears to be the sign of one of the greatest events of our century—I mean the presence of the Latin American nations in the front of the world stage; particularly, too, since the singular characteristic of this common action of Mexico and France, as opposed to the axes and pacts formerly concluded to gain domination, is the fact that it is directed only to the benefit of our peoples and for the sake of progress, without harming anyone—in short, since it is created to serve the cause of peace.

In Basse-Terre, on March 20, 1964, De Gaulle drew the conclusions of his official visit to Mexico; he evoked the impulse to confidence he felt among the people as well as in official quarters, the impulse to friendship he had found in other foreign countries where he had had occasion, recently, to represent France:

From this I have concluded, and everyone has concluded with me, that the international situation of our country is more brilliant, more assured than it ever was. We are a great nation, as the entire world acknowledges.

This does not mean that we oppose those who do not threaten us, particularly those who are naturally our friends and our allies. It is their responsibility to adapt themselves to this new and for us very satisfying situation of French independence. But once they have done so, once they admit that France, too, can take initiatives, establish foreign policy, and exert action accordingly, there will no longer be the shadow of a cloud between us and them. This is their affair. We hope that they will acknowledge as much as soon as possible.

A touch too much satisfaction, a touch too much impertinence, perhaps. But who can be surprised that De Gaulle crows, after the affronts he endured from our allies in London, in Algiers, in Paris itself, where he found himself installed in August 1944 without his government's having yet been recognized! As for the greatness of which he has spoken so much, of which he has given us more than an expression, an image, an image admired by our friends and adversaries alike, he declared, with simple pride, at the end of the same speech in Basse-Terre:

Occasionally someone says: "Oh, that's De Gaulle talking about greatness. . . ." Yes, it is. France has need of it. Our fathers, in every age, could do something meaningful, something important, only if they desired it to be great. And that is where we are today as well. Moreover, this is not the costliest of policies. The costliest policy, the most ruinous policy, is to ask something of everyone and never to obtain it.

Henceforth, France no longer asks; she gives. And the greatness of France, for De Gaulle, is above all her mission of co-operation and of promotion. He repeated this in Basse-Terre, as he would repeat it on March 21 in Cayenne, and on March 22 in Fort-de-France; as he had said it on that same March 20 at Pointe-à-Pitre, and in Mexico during the preceding days.

This is to the interest of France, and De Gaulle, a realist as always, continually reminds us of the fact. ("It is a fact: decolonization is in our interest and, consequently, our policy," he declared on April 19, 1961.) But this is also to the honor not of any one country, or even of Europe, but of the planet. This is what the general said during his journey to the French Antilles, on March 23, 1964, in his answer to Aimé Césaire, the Mayor of Fort-de-France and Deputy from Martinique:

What I have seen this morning was truly incomparable. In the demonstration of the people there was a contact among Frenchmen that transcended our persons, the circumstances, and the contingencies of the moment. This was, of course, moving for

the man who speaks to you now and comforting for our people. I
have heard, Monsieur le Maire, what you said of the history of
Martinique. Yes, there are in the history of peoples, and especially
in the history of our people, obstacles, ordeals that have been surmounted, and yet these ordeals might have been mortal. You
have known such ordeals.

The world today is complex, and the daily drama of this world
is, above and beyond all countries and all States, the drama of
man. The question facing us as Frenchmen is this: What can be
done to make the condition of mankind best, noblest, worthiest?
France has done her duty and will continue to do it vis-à-vis her
children—here with you and in the world, with the intention
of being loyal to her vocation and to her genius, which are always
human ones. France does not fear the judgment that her children,
wherever they may be and here in particular, pass upon her in the
depths of their hearts; and beyond any formulas, perhaps beyond
any coalitions, all her children feel that she is doing her duty. I
return to my country more convinced than ever of the prestige of
France. I am convinced that she is taking the right course. May
those who are her children remain with her! That is what she believes it is her duty to ask of them.

Thus we find, once again, that *contact of souls* between
France and De Gaulle, but the question is no longer one of
French policy alone. De Gaulle has evaded the questions
Aimé Césaire has just asked him, but he has elevated the
discussion: he has placed Martinique in the totality of
France and the totality of France in the world. Henceforth,
he will stress the responsibility of France not only to her
children, but to the free peoples whom "her vocation and
her genius" oblige her to furnish, to the limit of her capacity, with spiritual and material aid. Hence De Gaulle already spoke here less as a Frenchman or as a European,
than as a citizen of tomorrow's unified world.

I HAVE ASKED De Gaulle himself to tell us who De Gaulle is. And now I come back to my first sketch, and I confront it with the figure created before my eyes by the public statements of the general, the expression of his explicit thoughts, perhaps not of his ulterior motives. Must I revise my initial sketch? That is the whole question, at the moment of conclusion.

Actually, all the books written about De Gaulle the man resemble each other in the last chapter. All end with the same door open onto the unknown, the same throng of professional politicians, disappointed and uneasy, quivering with impatience as they wait for the hero's exit. As long as he is on the stage, the parliamentary game, as the French have played it, to their cost, for almost a century, remains suspended. If the institutions he has just given us take root, if he himself manages to stay at the helm for some time in the Élysée, or if he remains in the wings at Colombey to supervise developments, then a whole political generation on the Left will have been frustrated and deprived; and for the far Right, the story will have ended with the debâcle of the OAS.

The passions, avowed or repressed, that De Gaulle, alive and present, awakens in men's hearts would seem to doom to failure, at least in the realm of the absolute, his dream of "uniting France." The Frenchmen of De Gaulle's time do

not love one another any more than the Gauls of Caesar's
time loved one another. But De Gaulle has always known
that such unity exists only as an attempt ceaselessly interrupted, destroyed, and revived. It is enough if France's
institutions breast the current of hatred to allow the secretly divided nation to show at the prow of Europe the
countenance that resembles the image of her De Gaulle
has always cherished in his heart and in his mind.

What De Gaulle has understood is that the more France
exists as a nation, the more importantly she performs in
the world. The parrots of the Left denounced his nationalism, and the parrots of the Right screamed that he had
condemned us to solitude. But no sooner had the French nation emerged from its last two colonial wars than it recovered its rank and resumed its place, not by virtue of its
very reduced power, but simply because it was France.

Charles de Gaulle, upon his entrance into history, was
generally in conflict with the leader of England in arms, of
invincible Albion, and with the President of the United
States of America. And in so far as he embodied anything,
he embodied a defeated people who no longer existed as
a national power. Yet at that very moment, Charles de
Gaulle prevailed over his formidable partners. His least remark proves it: he kept before his eyes, at every moment
and everywhere at once, the battle being fought throughout
the world; but whereas the other two believed that France
was finished, an error that distorted their calculations (after twenty years the consequences are still making themselves felt), De Gaulle's act of faith in France made him
speak and act as if our disaster had been merely an episode,
and thereby allowed him to stand his ground against the
masters of the world and to yield nothing essential to them,
simply because he was in the right against them. He was
right to proclaim that France, momentarily crushed and
dishonored, remained: she constituted an inevitable don-
née which they would not dismiss from the solution to-

ward which they were heading. And he was right to say of
this France, henceforth and already free, henceforth and
already in combat: "La France, c'est moi!" although for
Roosevelt and even for Churchill this was the claim of a
madman.

Perhaps, at this moment, General de Gaulle believed that
France would one day resume her place beside her allies—
her true place, not the one she rather quickly obtained
when she occupied Germany and was present at the
enemy's surrender—the place that would assure her total
equality in every domain, and particularly on the atomic
level.

This ambition General de Gaulle must have abandoned
quite soon. If I have made only one allusion to the letter of
September 28, 1958, sent by the President of the French
Republic to the President of the United States, General
Eisenhower, and to Mr. Macmillan, proposing that the three
of them unite in an atomic directorate, it is not because the
importance of this letter has escaped me, but because to
my mind it is far from proving that in 1958 General de
Gaulle still believed that France could occupy that privileged place beside her great allies. Knowing men as he does
(and these two men in particular . . .), how could he have
doubted the refusal he would receive? Even if there had
been no other reasons than the jealousy of her European
allies, America would have had to dismiss the French
claim. And De Gaulle could not help knowing it.

In truth, he reckoned on this refusal—the refusal that was
to afford him an untried opportunity. This refusal meant
that General de Gaulle could at last bear witness before
the world that the world was no longer caught between two
great jaws. This was not a new policy he was devising, nor
was it a conception he had attempted to establish in the
realm of facts: this policy had been gradually revealed by
the facts themselves.

One of the most determined and severe adversaries of De Gaulle and of Gaullism, Claude Bourdet, has quite recently acknowledged as much: "De Gaulle," he writes, "by certain initiatives, conceived by him as simple means of influence and of 'greatness,' but taken in a period when he nevertheless possessed no major military means, has demonstrated to the world that the blocs are paralyzing each other, that there is no longer reason to be afraid and to cling to alliances, and also that military force is no longer, in this situation of paralysis, a condition of independence . . ."

It is not De Gaulle who has created, or even provoked, this state of affairs. He has been, in a sense, its midwife, because he became aware of it before the others, and because, thanks to the institutions the French have received from him, he happens to have been the first French political leader in a hundred years who has had his hands free, and whose decision is swayed by no imperative of domestic policy.

That is the point De Gaulle has reached in his history and in ours, the turning point where I must stop. It is a point where every Frenchman should pause to reflect. For the maintenance or the ruin of this policy will one day depend on the man chosen to replace De Gaulle—to replace him, or to continue him? That is the question, because the Gaullist approach can be continued. The method does not require genius. Thanks to De Gaulle, French foreign policy no longer obeys anything but its own necessity, and he has at the same time given us the institutions likely to safeguard that finally regained freedom. Even if he were not a candidate, his name would still be the center of the controversy in France. The stake of the electoral battle will be the institutions we have received from him. There will be a Gaullist candidate to defend them, facing a determined adversary who will not perhaps attack them openly, but pretend to remodel them, in the fashion of the last two Republics. At this final point where I suspend my inquiry, this is what seems clear to me: when De Gaulle is no longer here, he will still be here. And if it comes to a wager, I wager that it will once again be De Gaulle who will decide.

What else can I do, at this turning point I claim to have reached, but continue to observe my character in action, and gaze after him as long as possible; until the press is locked, can I not add a line, retouch a feature? This, then, is the last journal of my thought, kept while I observe De Gaulle here and now.

When De Gaulle returns from his Picardy tour, it strikes me that the perplexity of the public and the parties is at its height. No man has ever obliged the French to ask themselves so many questions whose answer depends on himself alone. This may irritate and even exasperate the parliamentarians of the old order: that the fate of the nation depends on the calculations, or the moods, of one brigadier general is more than they can endure, yet that is what they must endure, without finding any remedy for it.

But for De Gaulle himself, has "suspense" become a method of domestic politics, a method he has invented, or perfected? Actually, I am sure that initially he intended no malice by it. His pragmatism was applied here as on any other terrain: if he did not reveal his plans in advance, and did not make his projects known, it was because he did not know them himself and because they were, in a sense, the product of circumstances. De Gaulle, at the last second, could take an unexpected direction, one necessitated by the situation. Perhaps he has known only since yesterday, or even today, if he plans to continue *as planned*. Certainly De Gaulle has not deliberately resorted to suspense as a system, but I suspect and believe that he has ended up by taking a certain pleasure in it all the same.

And all the more pleasure the more he irritates and disconcerts his adversary. Thus he comes to emphasize what embarrasses even his friends: the fact that the fate of the

Republic depends on the whim of a citizen who, however great he may be, is only one of us. As Cassius says to Brutus: "When could they say till now that talk'd of Rome, That her wide walls encompass'd but one man?"

To which the answer is that they could not say so. I may have felt as much myself, but I call the immortal gods to witness—to speak like those Romans—that I do not hold General de Gaulle responsible for his solitude: it was born of the ruins of the two Republics that collapsed, one after the other, not so much under blows delivered from without as eroded by termites from within. The solitude of a man is not himself, it is the desert around him, and it is you who are responsible for this desert, and above all you men of a countless and ankylosed Left, whose paralysis derives largely from the fact that General de Gaulle has accomplished by himself, and by himself made into realities, what remained only aspirations and dreams among the politicians of the Left, subject as they were to the imperatives of the Right whenever they took the helm. I have difficulty believing in the good faith of the colleagues who reproach me for defending De Gaulle after having defended Mendès-France—whose honor is precisely to have initiated the policy which De Gaulle has carried through to its conclusion.

This would be the sufficient reason for their resentment, if there were not that other reason to which we must ceaselessly return and which can be put into a formula: *careers interrupted by a destiny*. And for my part, I believe that several of these careers deserved to become destinies in their turn, not by opposing De Gaulle, not by rising against De Gaulle, as Pierre Mendès-France imagined, but by enriching him with certain contributions that De Gaulle has not received from his training and that he has not found in his heritage.

Certainly, at first glance, for a Mendès-France (I am writing this ten years after his accession to the presidency of the

Council), the choice he made following the thirteenth of May seemed inevitable. Did there not have to be a head of the opposition, a thinking head, and precisely that of one of De Gaulle's first partisans? Pierre Mendès-France might at least have waited, might have kept himself in reserve. He chose, as soon as De Gaulle returned to power, to predict catastrophes. He made himself the prophet of a disaster that has not come to pass. In every realm where he predicted collapse, there has been recovery.

I am not so mad as to believe a politician capable of saying: "I was mistaken, we were mistaken: it is ourselves whom we have fought in De Gaulle. It is ourselves whom we have opposed, what it was our calling to do, and what De Gaulle has accomplished without us and against us. It is to *that* that we have said 'No'."

One can dream of a Mendès-France espousing the solitude that you blame on the man you have left alone. I imagine (what a lunatic dream!) a Mendès-France rallying to the camp of De Gaulle; then the Left would occupy a part of the terrain, the day the succession is open. It would have its place, the natural heir of a policy that belongs to it by right and that has always belonged to it.

This miracle will not take place. The Left will continue to offer a dispersed and divided front to the candidate inheriting the Gaullist mantle. But will there be only one? Will we not see the generals of Alexander devouring one another?

It is true that Mendès-France, even if he consented to say: "I made a mistake . . . ," would feel no less hostility and would manifest no less repugnance, at the mere thought of depending on one man, of being subject to one man . . . How strange it is! He did not feel humiliated, in the past, at depending on the parties leagued against him, at wasting the time such grave affairs demanded, at defending himself before hostile committees, at avoiding their snares and ambushes. Neither the *pics* nor the *banderillas* nor the final coup de grâce have ever humiliated this kind of bull. On the other hand, the meanders of a policy changing in appearance, shifting as circumstances themselves shift, the consent to a pilot, even to such a pilot as this one —that is what appears unendurable to a Mendès-France. The truth is that among the former consuls, none is willing to be the third, nor even the second; none is willing to be Lepidus, none is willing to be Lebrun.

Yet that is what I ask of them, and even of the best of them: is there one man among them who would dream of saying about him what Shakespeare's Octavius says of Antony: "We could not stall together In the whole world . . ." Let us leave aside the term "superiority," if it offends you. After all, each of you can, on particular points, surpass De Gaulle. We must return to the notion of solitude, for it is this solitude that ultimately horrifies you. I shall consider it, but no longer in the entirely physical, or even spiritual sense of the word: it is a historical solitude that is in question here; I mean that events, not during a brief period as in the case of Clemenceau or Churchill, but in the course of thirty years of a dramatic history, which still continues, could be mastered only by one man, and by that man alone, and on condition that those who surround him remain subordinate.

I am not expressing here a disputable opinion, for it is the opinion of history, and we have lived through it. I ask all those who fought in the Resistance, and I ask one of their wisest men, Pierre Mendès-France, and one of their most valorous, Claude Bourdet: "What would have become of you, or rather, what would have become of what you sought to save and to maintain throughout the inferno of enemy occupation, if De Gaulle's action had not been pursued beyond the Liberation? You must admit, everything would have been lost and ruined, and perhaps in dishonor. You

have blamed De Gaulle for the (admittedly murky) circumstances that in 1958 restored him to power at the penultimate moment. But it is because those circumstances
were urgent and because everything was at stake for the
Republic and for you, men of the Resistance, that De Gaulle
did not have to question himself, any more than a man
would hesitate to fling himself into the water, even into
the murkiest water, if he saw his mother and his brothers
drowning there. By instinct we pass quickly over this part
of the story which shames us. The pronunciamento belonged by right to the republics of Latin America. Our own
Republic had always held its pretorians on a short leash; it
won the two battles it fought against them: that of Boulangism and that of Dreyfus. Without De Gaulle, you might
have lost the third. In any case, you would have won it
only after a horrible settling of accounts, which De Gaulle,
and only De Gaulle, has spared you.

For it is a long way from the state of France in May 13,
1958, to what the Republic was in 1889 and 1896. Fascism,
nazism constitute not an epidemic disease, but a recurrent
one. If the colonels at the head of the specialized corps had
become the masters, even for a brief time, have you ever
envisaged the passions that would have been manifested,
satisfied, set loose? What a revenge for those who had escaped the "collaborationist" purges! I am not thinking so
much of the remark attributed to De Gaulle (apropos of
one of you): "Without me, he would have been hanged."
It is not so much our life he has saved, once again, but our
honor; for it was torture that then seemed likely to triumph
over those of us who had risen against it. And what its partisans were capable of, and how far they could have gone,
the OAS has demonstrated before our very eyes. If this
army had no longer been secret, but in control of the government and triumphant . . . such a state of affairs could
not have lasted, you say? I agree with you, of course. Nothing lasts against the facts. And the Algerian fact was modi-

fiable only by episodic crimes. Nevertheless we can ponder
what would have happened in Paris without De Gaulle.
One of the colonels, licking his chops, confided to Édouard
Corniglion-Molinier (who repeated it to me): "The first two
I'll have shot are Mauriac and Raymond Aron!" And when
Édouard Corniglion objected that De Gaulle would be
there to prevent such action: "De Gaulle?" the colonel protested, "De Gaulle? He's an old *schnock*." I imagine that the
colonel's ideas have altered.

But why should the ideas of Pierre Mendès-France—who
has ideas, ideas that have mattered and that still matter to
us—resist the scrutiny of what has happened since De
Gaulle's return to power? I am not crazy; I know perfectly
well that even if Pierre Mendès-France's nature was such
that he could acknowledge his mistake and admit as much
in the face of the world, he would remain no less suspicious
of the figure of De Gaulle, by an instinct inherited from his
radical ancestry.

The "republican belly"—those who have received it as a
heritage recognize each other and quickly unmask those
who speak as if they too possessed it. But it is of no use to
De Gaulle, a true republican from the time of Doumergue,
to have created and twice restored the Republic, to have
always appealed to it and to the principles on which it is
based. Under the Third Republic, which Marshal Mac-
Mahon and General Boulanger nearly overthrew, it was
enough to be a soldier to be suspect.

But above all, what De Gaulle has claimed to purge the
Republic of in order that it might become what he wanted
it to be constituted the very essence of the authentic Republic for the old republicans. The mere mention of the
referendum which is at the basis of the Gaullist institution
would once have sufficed to render a Frenchman suspect,
because it is scarcely to be distinguished from the plebiscite.
De Gaulle has dissipated the spell that for eighty years iden-

tified the notion of a Republic with that of an Assembly both sovereign and impotent, and of an executive power with its hands tied, its legs shackled.

Has De Gaulle been the author of this great change, or only its witness? To tell the truth, the two great wars were its direct cause. The disaster and the shame of the Second completed the disillusionment of the French. Marianne has once again become a little girl with an unknown fate, whose education lies ahead of her, a very different creature from the fat lady in the Phrygian cap, the radical and masonic Marianne in the caricatures of Dreyfus' day.

One fact, a very small fact but one that must have struck all the men of my age even if it has not even been noticed by our juniors, was the removal, without trumpet or drum, of Gambetta's statue from the Place du Carrousel. Before 1914, and even between the wars, this sacrilege would have been inconceivable, so intimately was the figure of Gambetta identified with republican principles. He who had seen Napoleon III and his horse knocked off their pedestal and thrown in the river so often, in so many provinces, has been knocked off in his turn, and not only in the Place du Carrousel, but also in Bordeaux, in the allées de Tourny, and no one knows in what dim vault he awaits an improbable resurrection.

What has become of the serpents that hissed over that equine head? The minister of the armies standing in the first row of a soldiers' pilgrimage in Lourdes astonishes the "republican belly" of the survivors of the Third Republic even more than the subsidies to our religious schools.

Why should the Consular Republic, as De Gaulle has conceived it, whose leader derives his power directly from the people, not be the true Republic—and in the name of what authority do you declare it to be suspect? In truth, it is less the principle that seems suspect to the old republicans than this general with Maurrassien training who has given it to us, and who has certainly taken the credit for twice saving the Republic. We cannot refuse him that: that he has twice picked it up out of the blood and mud where it was lying. And now he holds it—he even holds it tight—not, certainly, to offer it in homage to the Count of Paris, as some insinuate without believing it.

As a matter of fact, why has the Count of Paris become one of the characters of the play? Not because he has a part in it. But we finally glimpse him in the wings, surrounded by his family. "It was such a lovely family!" my grandmother sighed, regretting Louis-Philippe. Just what General de Gaulle thinks of the monarchy in absolute terms, we suspect. But we know that he is the one man in the world least capable of believing the monarchy can be imposed upon a people who made their revolution over a century ago.

The Count of Paris and what he embodies belong to the French hand of cards De Gaulle holds. It is the card that he will not play, that he will not have to play, but that he holds and that he considers as he considers any other institution inherited from an illustrious past. For De Gaulle the history of France is a tapestry each thread of which is precious, and there is no need to choose among the decorative figures still living there though no longer able to be of any use . . . But you never can tell. I don't know if De Gaulle, musing to himself, could ever have murmured this "you never can tell" apropos of the House of Orléans. That he might be capable of doing so would not prove that he is a man of the past, but quite the contrary that he is a free spirit, neither amazed nor alarmed by anything in this line of ideas, precisely because he is the captive of no tradition. The real traditionalists are minds of the Mendès-France type or of the Guy Mollet type, minds fixed once and for all in a certain conception of France, a France doomed to inflation, a France anarchic at home and subordinate abroad; minds convinced that everything will return to order, to that order of *theirs*, once General de Gaulle has left the stage, as if De Gaulle's victory over them did not come from the agreement of *his* mind with the world as it has become: a mind remaining free whereas theirs are subject to dogmas, and thereby bound.

After De Gaulle, how great a proportion of minds will he have liberated? That is the question. Has Gaullism imposed its structures upon an immobile and immutable France, or is it rather the sign of a change *in depth,* as we say? Actually, this is no more than a manner of speaking; I seem to suggest that there was a time when the world was not changing, was immobile, and that suddenly it began to move. But what we are living through today already existed, potentially, ten years ago, twenty years ago, and the proof of this lies in the divination, or rather the decipherment, that a De Gaulle has been able to make of the history he was interpreting even as he was creating it.

Everything has always moved around certain hardened, immobile minds. What is it, then, that makes the world today, which De Gaulle's adversaries no longer recognize, so different? It is no longer insanely for or against freedom, as it was in the time of our youth, depending upon whether we were on the Left or the Right. Technocracy corresponds to a state of affairs that has created a state of mind. It is no longer happiness that is a new idea in Europe but a certain notion of comfort, a comfort that has become obligatory. Indeed, the washing machine, television, and the second car have become the visible signs of a paradise that emerges during the three weeks of a vacation with pay: O luxuries that exist only in the notion one has of them, and in the memory one keeps of them! It is not De Gaulle who has invented this world, De Gaulle, the last knight errant of the old world. But alas! he is not often the knight errant of the western world when he speaks to us, when he addresses the French.

This great soul does not readily speak the language of the soul to Frenchmen who, one might think to hear him speak, have become not a people without a history but a people without problems, a people with no other concern in mind than never to have any again.

This De Gaulle of seventy-five, who has passed through the fire to come to us; this soldier wounded and buried alive, who has miraculously escaped the hecatomb of two wars; this man condemned to death, this victor around whom the bullets whistled in Notre-Dame, this prince surrounded by murderers—we should be entitled to hear at last from his lips a word that is no longer the word of the political leader or of the administrator responsible for the national patrimony . . .

But no one prompts De Gaulle on what he should say or do at this moment of his destiny. He alone knows why he remains on this frontier which he forbids himself to cross. There is in this proud man a deeply concealed humility, a kind of renunciation of loftiness. As if this albatross, like Baudelaire's, did not know he has a giant's wings! Ah, that speech to the young which De Gaulle has never made . . . But he knows why he has not made it.

It is up to us, as Christians, to recognize the trust for which we are more than ever responsible. In this world doomed to technological success and to the delights of paid vacations, every man heads for death and the best of Republics will, in this, make no difference to anyone. Half the world, the half that has received the Marxist gospel, is obligatorily atheist. But we—what are we? What do we believe? Have you nothing to say, no watchword to leave to these generations that follow on each others' heels and shoulder each other out of the way before being engulfed, one after the other, in the same darkness, or in the same light? Charles de Gaulle kneeling in the choir of Notre-Dame during the official ceremonies—what does he say to the Infinite Being?

It is not true that he has said, as some suppose, "The administration will follow!" but it is true that the administration has followed, and all has been for the best in the best of Republics. Nevertheless, nothing can keep this happy people from being seated in the shadow of death, as all peoples have been and will be. Have you nothing else to offer them but your gospel of effectiveness?

The half of the world condemned to State materialism has produced a race of men of which Gagarin is the type. Where are the heroes of that Christian humanism of which you are the depository? I see the difference clearly: there is not *one* French youth group upon which a truth controlled by the State is imposed—but various groups which mistrust and oppose one another. What you would say to the young Christians on your side would make the young Communists or the sons of the Radical Socialists of the Third Republic shrug their shoulders. When the issue is no longer, as it was in 1914 or 1940, the nation and its very existence to be preserved or maintained, and when a people is no longer united by that sacred duty, what remains for the leader concerned with uniting them except to avoid all the subjects that divide them and to keep to matters concerned with political science and economics, to the difficulties overcome, to the results achieved?

Perhaps a great politician, condemned not to raise his eyes above the terrain he is studying, ultimately loses the sense of what depends on a different knowledge. The human animal undergoes a conditioning, as in a pack where all the dogs are not trained for the same hunt and do not hunt the same game.

Yet take that Frenchman, that Frenchwoman whom De Gaulle addresses on television: it is not the neutrality of Indochina that interests them, or our independence of the United States, or merely—though this comes first—the cost of food, the rent, salaries, children, the problems of school and lycée . . . No, it is not only that either. Evil prowls through the lives of human beings. There is the woman who is unfaithful to her husband, the husband who betrays her, and ugliness and solitude for so many who have never been loved, and old age, disease, infirmity, and the enormous hovering shadow of cancer. And yet if there were a grid that you could simply fasten on top of this sinister collection of maledictions and suddenly a meaning would appear . . .

It is not De Gaulle's responsibility, you say, to give us that grid. But do Khrushchev and his successors hesitate to speak out as atheists, to appeal to their atheism as a source of action? There are not several De Gaulles in a generation. There is not even one in each generation. When he finally appears, we ask him for infinitely more than he gives, much though he has given. He shows us all the kingdoms of the earth, and we, we are advancing, we are marching toward another kingdom, which is not of this world.

You say: "These things do not concern human politics. There are two separate worlds, which the same laws do not govern. Politics concerns only reality . . ." But what is reality, if not what appears to us? Which brings everything back to a question of *lighting:* the same politics are brightened, or dimmed, at will. For example, we pride ourselves on the fact that for the first time in many years, France is at peace everywhere in the world, as if she had not been obliged to be. We boast of the fact that she has given independence to her Empire, as if decolonization had not been imposed from without. We congratulate ourselves on being the people who make the greatest sacrifices to aid the starving and the underdeveloped the world over, as if we were not invoking our own interest (rightly or wrongly understood), as if we were not flattering ourselves on making long-term investments in those countries!

Yes, all this is true, and there is no way to answer the cynic who makes us sing small. It is true, yet it is false. For it is also true that for the first time—in how many years!— the policy of France corresponds to what the nations expect of her. It is a fact; and what gives it greater bearing is that it is apparent in a France barely emerging from her two colonial wars (terrible wars, lost wars), and also that France is no longer a nation of the very first rank. What the world expects of us, what we have to give the world, neither the United States of America nor Soviet Russia can give it, despite their overwhelming power.

But it is as if we no longer knew this, or as if we pretended to know it no longer. Who will remind us of it, if not Charles de Gaulle? It remains for him to tell us again, opportunely and inopportunely, that greatness, what he calls greatness, is not identified with material power or technological success. If the diminished France of 1964 remains great, if her greatness, thanks to De Gaulle, has emerged intact from a shame she had not known before in a thousand years of history, then it is because our people have a principle within them—and whether we call it a "soul" or refer to a "vocation" is a matter of vocabulary. Soul, vocation derive from the Christian vocabulary familiar to me, and that is why I use them. This principle, whatever the name that designates it, may be despised by men today, yet it is this principle that makes the gestation of a united Europe so laborious. France has become France only to the degree to which Burgundy, Guienne, and the other provinces have been "depersonalized". A Breton soul, an Alsatian soul, a Basque soul still subsist. But most of the old regions of France lost their soul so that France might be born. Will the birth of the United States of Europe render such a sacrifice necessary? We know General de Gaulle's answer, and he will remind us of it until his last breath: his answer is that France, if she is no longer *the* great nation, remains the irreplaceable nation, and that to serve France is to serve the world.